The COMPLETE LAUGH-OUT-LOUD JOKES for KIDS

The COMPLETE LAUGH -OUT- LOUD JOKES *for* KIDS

* A 4-in-1 Collection *

ROB ELLIOTT

Revell

a division of Baker Publishing Group
Grand Rapids, Michigan

© 2010, 2012, 2013, 2014 by Robert E. Teigen

Published by Revell
a division of Baker Publishing Group
P.O. Box 6287, Grand Rapids, MI 49516-6287
www.revellbooks.com

Hardcover edition published 2016

ISBN 978-0-8007-2829-8

Previously published in four separate volumes:
Laugh-Out-Loud Jokes for Kids © 2010
Laugh-Out-Loud Animal Jokes for Kids © 2012
Knock-Knock Jokes for Kids © 2013
More Laugh-Out-Loud Jokes for Kids © 2014

Printed in the United States of America

The poem "Ode to a Cricket" is used by permission

17   18   19   20   21   22   7   6   5   4   3

CONTENTS

1

LAUGH -OUT- LOUD JOKES *for* KIDS

Q & A Jokes

Q: Why did the robber wash his clothes before he ran away with the loot?

A: He wanted to make a clean getaway.

Q: How does a skeleton call his friends?

A: On the tele-bone.

Q: What is the richest kind of air?

A: A millionaire.

Q: Who keeps the ocean clean?

A: The mermaid.

Q: Why did the invisible man turn down a job offer?

A: He just couldn't see himself doing it.

Q: Why did the skeleton drink eight glasses of milk every day?

A: Milk is good for the bones.

Q: Why did Johnny jump up and down before he drank his juice?

A: The carton said to "shake well before drinking."

Q: What is a baby's favorite reptile?

A: A rattlesnake.

Q: What does a snowman eat for breakfast?

A: Frosted Flakes.

Q: Where do generals keep their armies?

A: In their sleevies.

Q: How do you make a hot dog stand?

A: Take away its chair.

Q: What kind of balls don't bounce?

A: Eyeballs.

Q: Why can't you play hide-and-seek with mountains?

A: Because they're always peaking.

Q: What did the bride say when she dropped her bouquet?

A: "Whoopsy-Daisies."

Q: Why did Jimmy's parents scream when they saw his grades?

A: Because he had a bee on his report card.

Q: What do you call a stick that won't do anything you want?

A: A stick-in-the-mud.

Q: What do you get when you cross a pig and a centipede?

A: Bacon and legs.

Q: What do you get when you cross a tiger and a snowman?

A: Frostbite!

Q: What is a duck on the Fourth of July?

A: A fire-quacker.

Q: Why did the credit card go to jail?

A: It was guilty as charged.

Q: What would we get if we threw all the books in the ocean?

A: A title wave!

Q: What do you call a liar on the phone?

A: A telephony.

Q: What do peanut butter and jelly do around the campfire?

A: They tell toast stories.

Q: What did the baker say when he found the dough he'd lost?

A: "That's just what I kneaded!"

Q: Why did the flashlight, the camera, and the remote-controlled car attend the funeral?

A: They were grieving the dead batteries.

Q: Why wouldn't the team play with the third basketball?

A: Because it was an odd ball.

Q: Where do electric bills like to go on vacation?

A: I-Owe-A (Iowa).

Q: **Why did the queen go to the dentist?**

A: To get crowns on her teeth.

Q: **How did the lobster get to the ocean?**

A: By shell-icopter.

Q: **When does the road get angry?**

A: When someone crosses it.

Q: **Why was the king only a foot tall?**

A: Because he was a ruler.

Q: **What did the robber say when he stole from the bookstore?**

A: "I had better book it out of here."

Q: **Why did Sally's computer keep sneezing?**

A: It had a virus.

Q: **When do doctors get mad?**

A: When they lose their patients (patience).

Q: **Why did Jimmy throw the clock out the window?**

A: He wanted to see time fly.

Q: What language does a billboard speak?

A: Sign language.

Q: Why didn't the girl trust the ocean?

A: There was something fishy about it.

Q: What do you call four bullfighters in quicksand?

A: Cuatro sinko.

Q: How did the baseball player lose his house?

A: He made his home run.

Q: Who was the only person in the Bible without a father?

A: Joshua, because he was the son of Nun (none).

Q: Why did the man put his money in the freezer?

A: He wanted some cold hard cash.

Q: What did the one-dollar bill say to the ten-dollar bill?

A: You don't make any cents (sense).

Q: What happens when race car drivers eat too much?

A: They get Indy-gestion.

Q: Why do baseball pitchers stay away from caves?
A: They don't like bats.

Q: What kind of tree has the best bark?
A: A dogwood.

Q: What kind of makeup do pirate girls wear?
A: Ship gloss.

Q: When do you need Chapstick in the garden?
A: When you're planting the tulips (two lips).

Q: Why did the trees take a nap?
A: For rest (forest).

Q: What is a zucchini's favorite game?
A: Squash.

Q: Why wouldn't the lion eat the clown?
A: He tasted funny.

Q: What kinds of hats do you wear on your legs?
A: Knee caps.

Q: How do you reach a book in an emergency?

A: Call its pager.

Q: Who helped the monster go to the ball?

A: Its scary godmother.

Q: Why did the banana wear sunscreen at the beach?

A: It didn't want to peel.

Q: Where does a ship go when it's not feeling well?

A: To see the dock-tor.

Q: Why was the nose feeling sad?

A: It was tired of getting picked on.

Q: What did the elevator say to its friend?

A: "I think I'm coming down with something."

Q: Why did Billy have a hot dog in his shoe?

A: It was a foot-long.

Q: What gets wet while it dries?

A: A towel.

Q: How did the farmer fix his jeans?

A: With a cabbage patch.

Q: What do you call a silly doorbell?

A: A ding-dong.

Q: What did the sock say to the foot?

A: "Shoe!"

Q: When do you stop at green and go on red?

A: When you're eating a watermelon.

Q: What did one tube of glue say to the other?

A: "Let's stick together."

Q: What did one wall say to the other?

A: "Let's meet at the corner!"

Q: Did you hear about the red ship and blue ship that collided?

A: All the sailors were marooned.

Q: Why did the girl need a ladder to go to school?

A: Because it was high school.

Q: What do sea monsters eat?

A: Fish and ships.

Q: What does a computer do when it's tired?

A: It crashes.

Q: What did the tooth fairy use to fix her wand?

A: Toothpaste.

Q: Why did the computer get glasses?

A: To improve his web sight.

Q: What stays in the corner but travels all over the world?

A: A stamp.

Q: What did the computer say when it fell into quicksand?

A: "Help me! I'm syncing!"

Q: What do you get when you have two doctors at once?

A: Pair-a-medics.

Q: What should you do when you get in a jam?

A: Grab some bread and peanut butter.

Q: How can you go surfing in the kitchen?

A: On a micro-wave.

Q: Why was everyone looking up at the ceiling and cheering?

A: They were ceiling fans.

Q: Why did the cowboy go out and buy a wiener dog?

A: Because someone told him to "get a *long*, little doggie."

Q: What is a trombone's favorite playground equipment?

A: The slide.

Q: How can you keep someone in suspense?

A: I'll tell you later.

Q: What happened to the beans when they showed up late to work?

A: They got canned.

Q: Why can't you take anything balloons say seriously?

A: They're always full of hot air.

Q: What happens when you phone a clown three times?

A: You get a three-ring circus.

Q: What do you get when you have breakfast with a centipede?

A: Pancakes and legs.

Q: What do you call someone who is afraid of picnics?

A: A basket case.

Q: How does an Eskimo fix his broken toys?

A: With igloo.

Q: What kind of flowers are great friends?

A: Rose buds.

Q: What do you get when you cross a tuba, a drum, and a spare tire?

A: A rubber band.

Q: Why did the lady sing lullabies to her purse?

A: She wanted a sleeping bag.

Q: What did the orange say to the banana when they were looking for the apple?

A: Keep your eyes peeled.

Q: Did you hear about the teacher who was cross-eyed?

A: She couldn't control her pupils.

Q: **What kinds of teeth cost money?**

A: Buck teeth.

Q: **What do you call a dentist who cleans an alligator's teeth?**

A: Crazy!

Q: **If a snake married an undertaker, what would they embroider on their towels?**

A: Hiss and Hearse (his and hers).

Q: **What is the difference between boogers and broccoli?**

A: Kids won't eat their broccoli.

Q: **What do elves learn in kindergarten?**

A: The elf-abet.

Q: **Why did the golfer wear two pairs of pants?**

A: In case he got a hole in one.

Q: **Why didn't the skeleton go to the ball?**

A: He had no body to dance with.

Q: **What kind of beans don't grow in a garden?**

A: Jelly beans.

Q: Why can't a nose be twelve inches long?

A: If it was, then it would be a foot.

Q: When does your dinner never get hot?

A: When it's chili.

Q: Why did the boys shoot their BB guns in the air?

A: They wanted to shoot the breeze.

Q: Why were the Cheerios scared of the man?

A: He was a cereal killer.

Q: Why did the baseball player go to jail?

A: He stole second base.

Q: Why couldn't the twelve-year-old go to the pirate movie?

A: It was rated arrrgh.

Q: How did Benjamin Franklin feel about discovering electricity?

A: He was shocked.

Q: What do you call cheese that doesn't belong to you?

A: Nacho cheese.

Q: How much did the butcher charge for his venison?
A: A buck.

Q: What does a rain cloud wear under its clothes?
A: Thunderwear.

Q: How did Thomas Edison invent the lightbulb?
A: He got a bright idea.

Q: Why did the lettuce win the race?
A: He was a head.

Q: Where did the most talkative people in the Bible live?
A: Babylon (babble on).

Q: Why was the broom late for school?
A: It over-swept.

Q: What did the alien say to the flower bed?
A: "Take me to your weeder."

Q: What kind of button won't you find at a sewing store?
A: A belly button.

Q: Why did the lady throw her butter out the window?

A: She wanted to see a butterfly.

Q: Why did the ninja go to the doctor?

A: He had kung-flu.

Q: What did the grape do when the lemon asked for a kiss?

A: It puckered up.

Q: Why couldn't the monster go to sleep?

A: It was afraid there were kids under the bed.

Q: How long does it take to count four times infinity?

A: Four-ever.

Q: Who fills your tank at the gas station?

A: Philip (fill up).

Q: What is an alien's favorite kind of candy?

A: A Mars bar.

Q: How do you get a skeleton to laugh out loud?

A: Tickle its funny bone.

Q: What do you take before every meal?
A: You take a seat.

Q: What did the mother corn say to her children?
A: "Don't forget to wash behind your ears."

Q: Did you hear about the actor who fell through the floor?
A: It was just a stage he was going through.

Q: What did the tomato say to the mushroom?
A: "You look like a fungi."

Q: Why are babies so good at basketball?
A: Because they like to dribble.

Teacher: Name two days of the week that start with a "t."
Student: Today and tomorrow.

Teacher: Billy, you missed school yesterday.
Billy: Well, to tell you the truth, I didn't miss it that much at all.

Fred: Today the teacher was yelling at me for something I didn't do.

Mike: What was that?

Fred: My homework.

Q: Why did the cookie complain about feeling sick?

A: He was feeling crummy.

Q: Why is spaghetti the smartest food there is?

A: It always uses its noodle.

Q: What do you call a student who never turns in his math homework on time?

A: A calcu-later.

Q: How did the karate teacher greet his students?

A: "Hi-Yah!"

Q: Why did the bed wear a disguise?

A: It was undercover.

Q: What do you call a boomerang that doesn't come back?

A: A stick.

Q: When do pine trees like to do embroidery?

A: When they do needlepoint.

Q: What is a baby's motto?

A: If at first you don't succeed, cry, cry again.

Q: Where do you keep your jokes?

A: In a giggle box.

Q: Why did the lady wear a helmet every time she ate?

A: She was on a crash diet.

Q: Why did the hot dog turn down the chance to star in a movie?

A: None of the roles (rolls) were good enough.

Josh: **Did you hear about the restaurant on the moon?**

Anna: What about it?

Josh: **It has great food but no atmosphere.**

Q: What do you call a fairy that doesn't take a bath?

A: Stinkerbell.

Q: What did one candle say to the other?

A: "Do you want to go out tonight?"

Q: What is a plumber's favorite vegetable?

A: A leek.

Q: How did the French fry propose to the hamburger?

A: He gave her an onion ring.

Q: What has four legs and one head but only one foot?

A: A bed.

Q: What do potatoes wear to bed?

A: Yammies.

Q: What fruit teases people a lot?

A: A bana na na na na na!

Q: Why was the metal wire so upset?

A: It was getting all bent out of shape over nothing.

Q: What do you call the story of the three little pigs?

A: A pigtail.

Q: What did the peanut butter say to the bread?

A: "Quit loafing around."

Q: What did the bread say back to the peanut butter?

A: "I think you're nuts."

Q: What kind of lights did Noah use on the ark?

A: Flood lights.

Q: How did the orange get into the crowded restaurant?

A: He squeezed his way in.

Q: Why can't the bank keep a secret?

A: It has too many tellers.

Q: Why was the sewing machine so funny?

A: It kept everyone in stitches.

Q: Why did the hamburger always lose the race?

A: It could never ketchup.

Q: How do you punish a naughty eyeball?

A: Give it fifty lashes.

Q: Why was the rope so stressed out?

A: It was getting itself all tied in knots.

Q: What did the math book say to the psychiatrist?

A: "Would you like to hear my problems?"

Q: What do you call a fossil that never does any work?

A: A lazy bones.

Q: What did the pen say to the pencil?

A: "You're sure looking sharp today."

Q: What is green and can sing?

A: Elvis Parsley.

Q: Why didn't the string ever win a race?

A: It was always tied.

Q: What is the best food to eat when you're scared?

A: I scream.

Q: How do you get a tissue to dance?

A: Put a little boogie in it.

Q: What did the tree say to the flower?

A: "I'm rooting for you."

Q: What is the craziest way to travel?

A: By loco-motive.

Q: What did the paper say to the pencil?

A: "You've got a good point."

Q: What is the cheapest way to travel?

A: By sale-boat.

Q: Who are the cleanest people in the choir?

A: The soap-ranos.

Q: What is the noisiest game you can play?

A: Racket-ball.

Q: What did the earthquake say to the tornado?

A: "Don't look at me, it's not my fault."

Q: What did the tree say to the lumberjack?

A: "Leaf me alone!"

Q: Why was it so hot in the stadium after the baseball game?

A: All the fans left.

Q: Why did the ice cream cone become a reporter?

A: He wanted to get the scoop.

Q: What did the ice cream cone ride to the store?

A: A fudge-cycle.

Q: What kind of poles can swim?

A: Tadpoles.

Q: Why wouldn't the teddy bear eat anything?

A: He was already stuffed.

Q: How does a gingerbread man make his bed?

A: With a cookie sheet.

Q: What do you get when you cross an elephant with Darth Vader?

A: An ele-Vader.

Q: What do cowboys like on their salad?

A: Ranch dressing.

Q: Why was the elf crying?

A: He stubbed his mistle-toe.

Q: How do you make an orange giggle?

A: Tickle its navel.

Q: What kind of candy is never on time?

A: Choco-late.

Q: What kind of music does a boulder like?

A: Rock-n-roll.

Q: What did the mommy rope say to the baby rope?

A: "Don't be knotty."

Q: What do you call a monster with a high IQ?

A: Frank-Einstein.

Q: What did the turkey say to the ham?

A: "Nice to meat you!"

Q: Why was the Incredible Hulk so good at gardening?

A: He had a green thumb.

Q: What did the pool say to the lake?

A: "Water you doing here?"

Q: What did the cake say to the knife?

A: "Do you want a piece of me?"

Q: What was the math teacher's favorite dessert?

A: Pi.

Q: What does bread wear to bed?

A: Jam-mies.

Q: Who earns a living driving their customers away?

A: Taxi drivers.

Q: What did the lumberjack say to the tree?

A: "I have an axe to grind with you."

Customer: Excuse me, waiter, but is there spaghetti on the menu?

Waiter: No, but I believe we have some in the kitchen.

Q: What was the best time of day in the Middle Ages?

A: Knight-time.

Q: What is the fastest peanut butter in the world?

A: Jiffy.

Q: Why was the baseball player a bad sport?

A: He stole third base and then went home.

Q: Where do lumberjacks keep their pigs?

A: In their hog cabin.

Q: What is the difference between a football player and a dog?

A: A football player has a whole uniform, but a dog only pants.

Q: Why was the science teacher angry?

A: He was a mad scientist.

Q: Why was the tree excited about the future?

A: It was ready to turn over a new leaf.

Q: What do trees eat for breakfast?

A: Oakmeal.

Q: What is worse than finding a worm in your apple?

A: Finding *half* of a worm in your apple!

Q: Why did Cinderella get kicked out of the soccer game?

A: She ran away from the ball.

Q: What is a race car driver's favorite meal?

A: Fast food.

Q: What does a skipper eat for breakfast?

A: Captain Crunch.

Q: If April showers bring May flowers, what do Mayflowers bring?

A: Pilgrims.

Q: What runs around the football field but never moves?

A: A fence.

Q: Why was the jelly so stressed out?

A: It was spread too thin.

Awesome Animal Jokes

Q: A cowboy arrives at the ranch on a Sunday, stays three days, and leaves on Friday. How is that possible?

A: The horse's name is Friday.

Q: What do you call a bear standing in the rain?

A: A drizzly bear.

Q: What happened when the spider got a new car?

A: It took it for a spin.

Q: Why did the cow become an astronaut?

A: So it could walk on the moooo-n.

Q: Where do shrimp go if they need money?

A: The prawn shop.

Q: Why did the boy canary make the girl canary pay for her own meal on their date?

A: Because he was cheep.

Q: Why do flamingos stand on one leg?

A: If they lifted the other leg, they'd fall over.

Q: What do you get when you cross a fish and a kitten?

A: A purr-anha.

Q: How are fish and music the same?

A: They both have scales.

Q: What did the mother lion say to her cubs before dinner?

A: "Shall we prey?"

Q: What's worse than raining cats and dogs?

A: Hailing taxi cabs.

Q: Why are pigs so bad at football?

A: They're always hogging the ball.

Q: What do you call a lion whose car breaks down five miles before he gets to the zoo?

A: A cab.

Q: **What is a whale's favorite game?**

A: Swallow the leader.

Q: **What do you call bears with no ears?**

A: B.

Q: **Why is it hard to trust what a baby chick is saying?**

A: Talk is cheep.

Q: **Why did the clown visit the aquarium?**

A: To see the clown fish.

Q: **What is the best way to communicate with a fish?**

A: Drop it a line!

Q: **Why couldn't the elephants go swimming at the pool?**

A: They were always losing their trunks.

Q: **Why did the sparrow go to the library?**

A: It was looking for bookworms.

Q: **What did the dog say when he rubbed sandpaper on his tail?**

A: "Ruff, ruff."

Q: What kind of sea creature hates all the others?

A: A hermit crab.

Q: Where can you go to see mummies of cows?

A: The Mooseum of History.

Q: What kind of seafood tastes great with peanut butter?

A: Jellyfish.

Q: Why is it easy to play tricks on lollipops?

A: They're suckers.

Q: Why did the cat get detention at school?

A: Because he was a cheetah.

Q: Where do bees come from?

A: Stingapore and Beelivia.

Q: Why couldn't the polar bear get along with the penguin?

A: They were polar opposites.

Q: What did the rooster say to the hen?

A: "Don't count your chickens before they hatch."

Q: What happens when a cat eats a lemon?

A: You get a sourpuss.

Q: What language do pigs speak?

A: Swine language.

Q: What do cars and elephants have in common?

A: They both have trunks.

Q: What is a bat's motto?

A: Hang in there.

Q: What do you get when you cross a rabbit and frog?

A: A bunny ribbit.

Q: What do you get when you cross a dog and a daisy?

A: A collie-flower.

Q: What does a cat say when it's surprised?

A: "Me-WOW!"

Q: Why did the parakeet go to the candy store?

A: To get a tweet.

Q: What do you have if your dog can't bark?

A: A hush-puppy.

Q: Why do seagulls fly over the sea?

A: Because if they flew over the bay they'd be bagels.

Q: Why did Rover beat up Fido?

A: Because Rover was a Boxer.

Q: What do you get when an elephant sneezes?

A: You get out of the way!

Q: What is the craziest bird in the world?

A: The coo-coo bird.

Q: What is the dumbest bird in the world?

A: The do-do bird.

Q: What do you get when your dog makes your breakfast?

A: You get pooched eggs.

Q: Why did the horse wake up with a headache?

A: Because at bedtime he hit the hay.

Q: **What do trees and dogs have in common?**
A: They both have bark.

Q: **What kind of bees never die?**
A: Zom-bees.

Q: **What do you call a lazy kangaroo?**
A: A pouch potato.

Q: **What happened when the sharks raced each other?**
A: They tide (get it . . . they tied).

Q: **Why couldn't the goats get along?**
A: They kept butting heads.

Q: **What type of bat is silly?**
A: A ding-bat.

Q: **When do fireflies get uptight?**
A: When they need to lighten up.

Q: **Why do rhinos have so many wrinkles?**
A: Because they're so hard to iron.

Q: Where did the turtle fill up his gas tank?

A: At the shell station.

Q: Why did the pony get sent to his room without supper?

A: He wouldn't stop horsing around.

Q: What is a snake's favorite subject in school?

A: World hiss-tory.

Q: What kind of animal is related to a computer?

A: A ram.

Q: What do you call an insect that complains all the time?

A: A grumble-bee.

Q: Why were the deer, the chipmunk, and the squirrel laughing so hard?

A: Because the owl was a hoot!

Q: What do you call a monkey who won't behave?

A: A bad-boon.

Q: What kind of bugs read the dictionary?

A: Spelling bees.

Q: What do you call a calf that gets into trouble?
A: Grounded beef.

Q: What do you call a dinosaur who's scared all the time?
A: A nervous Rex.

Q: What do you call a polar bear in Hawaii?
A: Lost!

Q: Where do you take a sick bumblebee?
A: To the wasp-ital.

Q: Who made the fish's wishes come true?
A: Its fairy cod-mother.

Q: Where do pigs go for a rest?
A: To their ham-mock.

Q: What do you get if a cow is in an earthquake?
A: A milkshake.

Q: How does a farmer count his cattle?
A: With a cow-culator.

Q: Why does a milking stool only have three legs?

A: Because the cow has the udder one.

Q: Where do rabbits go after their wedding?

A: They go on their bunny-moon.

Joe: There were ten cats on a boat and one jumped off. How many were left?

Jack: I don't know, Joe. I guess nine?

Joe: No, there were none! They were all a bunch of copy cats.

Q: How come hyenas are so healthy?

A: Because laughter is the best medicine.

Q: Why don't Dalmatians like to take baths?

A: They don't like to be spotless.

Q: What do you get when sheep do karate?

A: Lamb chops.

Q: Why did the rooster go to the doctor?

A: It had the cock-a-doodle-flu.

Q: What do birds do before they work out?

A: They do their worm-ups.

Q: What kind of insects are bad at football?

A: Fumblebees.

Q: What do you call a deer with no eyes?

A: No eye deer (no idea).

Q: Why is it so easy for an elephant to get a job?

A: Because it will work for peanuts.

Q: What did the tiger say to her cubs when they wanted to go out and play?

A: "Be careful—it's a jungle out there!"

Q: Why did the monkey almost get fired?

A: It took him a while to get into the swing of things.

Q: Why is the snail one of the strongest creatures in the world?

A: It can carry its house on its back.

Q: What do you get when you cross a bear with a forest?

A: You get fur trees.

Q: Why did the elephant cross the road?

A: It's an elephant, so who's going to stop him?

Q: What is a frog's favorite flower?

A: A croak-us.

Q: How do you keep a dog from barking in the backseat of the car?

A: Put him in the front seat of the car.

Q: What do you get when you cross a monkey and a peach?

A: You get an ape-ricot.

Q: How do you greet a frog?

A: "Wart's up?"

Knock-Knock Jokes

Knock knock.
> Who's there?

Butter.
> Butter who?

**I butter not tell you—it's a
secret.**

Knock knock.
> Who's there?

Wendy.
> Wendy who?

**Wendy you think we'll be
done with these knock
knock jokes?**

Knock knock.
> Who's there?

Hailey.
> Hailey who?

**Hailey a cab so I can go
home.**

Knock knock.
> Who's there?

Wayne.
> Wayne who?

**The Wayne is really coming
down, so open the door!**

Knock knock.
   Who's there?
Weasel.
   Weasel who?
**Weasel be late if you don't
   hurry up.**

Knock knock.
   Who's there?
Raymond.
   Raymond who?
**Raymond me to go to the
   store to get some milk
   and eggs.**

Knock knock.
   Who's there?
Nose.
   Nose who?
**I nose a lot more knock
   knock jokes if you want
   to hear them.**

Knock knock.
   Who's there?
Hannah.
   Hannah who?
**Hannah me some of those
   apples, I'm hungry!**

Knock knock.
   Who's there?
Little old lady.
   Little old lady who?
**I didn't know you could
   yodel!**

Knock knock.
   Who's there?
Olive.
   Olive who?
**Olive you. Do you love me
   too?**

Knock knock.
   Who's there?
Eileen.
   Eileen who?
**I'm so tall, Eileen over to get
   through the door.**

Knock knock.
   Who's there?
Les.
   Les who?
**Les cut the small talk and let
   me in.**

Knock knock.
 Who's there?
Brett.
 Brett who?
Brett you don't know who
 this is!

Knock knock.
 Who's there?
Bacon.
 Bacon who?
I'm bacon a cake for your
 birthday.

Knock knock.
 Who's there?
Irish.
 Irish who?
Irish you'd let me in.

Knock knock.
 Who's there?
Ashley.
 Ashley who?
Ashley I changed my mind,
 and I don't want to
 come in.

Knock knock.
 Who's there?
Italy.
 Italy who?
Italy a shame if you don't
 open this door!

Knock knock.
 Who's there?
Alda.
 Alda who?
Alda kids like my knock
 knock jokes.

Knock knock.
 Who's there?
Gwen.
 Gwen who?
Gwen do you think we can
 get together?

Knock knock.
 Who's there?
Francis.
 Francis who?
Francis next to Spain.

Knock knock.
Who's there?
Cook.
Cook who?
Are you as crazy as you sound?

Knock knock.
Who's there?
Juno.
Juno who?
Juno it's me, so let me in now!

Knock knock.
Who's there?
Alex.
Alex who?
Alex plain later, now let me in!

Knock knock.
Who's there?
Gladys.
Gladys who?
Aren't you Gladys is the last knock knock joke?

Knock knock.
Who's there?
Joanna.
Joanna who?
Joanna come out and play?

Knock knock.
Who's there?
Archie.
Archie who?
Archie going to let me in?

Knock knock.
Who's there?
Robin.
Robin who?
Robin a bank is against the law.

Knock knock.
Who's there?
Duncan.
Duncan who?
Duncan cookies in milk tastes good.

Knock knock.
Who's there?
Pastor.
Pastor who?
**Pastor potatoes. I'm
hungry!**

Knock knock.
Who's there?
Carson.
Carson who?
**Carson the freeway drive
really fast.**

Knock knock.
Who's there?
Ben.
Ben who?
**I've Ben gone a lot lately
and came by to see you.**

Knock knock.
Who's there?
Doug.
Doug who?
**I Doug deep and still
couldn't find my keys.
Please let me in!**

Knock knock.
Who's there?
Aldon.
Aldon who?
**When you're Aldon with
dinner can you come
out and play?**

Knock knock.
Who's there?
House.
House who?
House it going for you?

Knock knock.
Who's there?
Arlo.
Arlo who?
**Arlo temperature is making
me cold. Please let me
in!**

Knock knock.
Who's there?
Ben.
Ben who?
**I haven't Ben over to visit in
a long time.**

Knock knock.
Who's there?
Mia.
Mia who?
Mia hand is killing me from all this knocking. Will you please let me in?

Knock knock.
Who's there?
Anna.
Anna who?
Anna chance you'll let me in? It's cold out here!

Knock knock.
Who's there?
Samantha.
Samantha who?
Can you give me Samantha to my questions?

Knock knock.
Who's there?
Lee.
Lee who?
I'm lone Lee without you. Please let me in!

Knock knock.
Who's there?
Ya.
Ya who?
Giddyup, cowboy!

Knock knock.
Who's there?
Cameron.
Cameron who?
Is the Cameron? I want to take a picture.

Knock knock.
Who's there?
Stan.
Stan who?
Stan back because I'm going to break down the door!

Knock knock.
Who's there?
Ice.
Ice who?
It would be really ice to see you, so please open the door.

Knock knock.
Who's there?
Eyes.
Eyes who?
Eyes better come in before I catch a cold.

Knock knock.
Who's there?
Ada.
Ada who?
I Ada lot for lunch, so now I'm really full.

Knock knock.
Who's there?
Dewey.
Dewey who?
Dewey have to go to school today?

Knock knock.
Who's there?
Peas.
Peas who?
Peas, can you come out and play?

Knock knock.
Who's there?
Fanny.
Fanny who?
If Fanny body asks, I'm not home.

Knock knock.
Who's there?
Hugo.
Hugo who?
Hugo first and I'll go second.

Knock knock.
Who's there?
Megan.
Megan who?
You're Megan me crazy with all of these knock knock jokes.

Knock knock.
Who's there?
Owen.
Owen who?
I'm Owen you a lot of money, but I'll pay you back soon!

Knock knock.
>Who's there?

Lucas.
>Lucas who?

Lucas in the eye and tell us
>you don't want to hear
>another knock knock
>joke!

Knock knock.
>Who's there?

Luke.
>Luke who?

You Luke like you want to
>hear another knock
>knock joke!

Knock knock.
>Who's there?

Quack.
>Quack who?

You quack me up with all
>these knock knock
>jokes.

Knock knock.
>Who's there?

Sadie.
>Sadie who?

If I Sadie magic word will
>you let me in?

Knock knock.
>Who's there?

Queen.
>Queen who?

I had a bath, so I'm queen as
>a whistle!

Knock knock.
>Who's there?

Baby Al.
>Baby Al who?

Baby Al will, baby Al won't.

Knock knock.
>Who's there?

Canoe.
>Canoe who?

Canoe come out and play?

Knock knock.
Who's there?
Oldest.
Oldest who?
Oldest knocking is giving
me a headache.

Knock knock.
Who's there?
Woody.
Woody who?
Woody like to hear another
knock knock joke?

Knock knock.
Who's there?
B.C.
B.C. who?
I'll B.C.-ing you soon.

Knock knock.
Who's there?
Weed.
Weed who?
Weed better go home now
for dinner.

Knock knock.
Who's there?
Dawn.
Dawn who?
Dawn mess around, or I'm
leaving!

Knock knock.
Who's there?
Rockefeller.
Rockefeller who?
Rockefeller in his cradle,
and he'll go right to
sleep.

Knock knock.
Who's there?
Dora.
Dora who?
A Dora is between us, so
open up!

Knock knock.
Who's there?
Braden.
Braden who?
Are you busy Braden your
hair, or will you open
the door?

Knock knock.
  Who's there?
Hannah.
  Hannah who?
Hannah over the keys so I
  can open this door!

Knock knock.
  Who's there?
Gary.
  Gary who?
Gary me inside—my legs
  are tired.

Knock knock.
  Who's there?
I don't know.
  I don't know who?
I don't know who either, so
  open the door and find
  out.

Knock knock.
  Who's there?
Beth.
  Beth who?
I didn't sneeze!

Knock knock.
  Who's there?
Shelby.
  Shelby who?
Shelby coming around the
  mountain when she
  comes!

Knock knock.
  Who's there?
Howl.
  Howl who?
Howl we get away from
  all these knock knock
  jokes?

Knock knock.
  Who's there?
Water.
  Water who?
Water you doing at my
  house?

Knock knock.
  Who's there?
Vera.
  Vera who?
Vera few people think these
  jokes are funny.

Knock knock.
Who's there?
Garden.
Garden who?
Stop garden the door and let me in!

Knock knock.
Who's there?
Willie.
Willie who?
Willie tell us more knock knock jokes?

Knock knock.
Who's there?
Annie.
Annie who?
Annie reason you're not opening the door?

Knock knock.
Who's there?
Moe.
Moe who?
Moe knock knock jokes, please.

Knock knock.
Who's there?
Dozen.
Dozen who?
Dozen anyone ever open the door?

Knock knock.
Who's there?
Ernest.
Ernest who?
Ernest is full of chicken eggs.

Knock knock.
Who's there?
Dragon.
Dragon who?
These jokes are dragon on and on.

Knock knock.
Who's there?
Taylor.
Taylor who?
Taylor brother to pick up his toys.

Knock knock.
  Who's there?
Dewy.
  Dewy who?
**Dewy get to hear more
  knock knock jokes?**

Knock knock.
  Who's there?
Lettuce.
  Lettuce who?
**Lettuce in and you'll find
  out.**

Knock knock.
  Who's there?
Collette.
  Collette who?
**Collette crazy, but I'd like to
  come in and see you.**

Knock knock.
  Who's there?
Achoo.
  Achoo who?
Achoo my gum every day.

Knock knock.
  Who's there?
Juicy.
  Juicy who?
**Juicy any monsters under
  my bed?**

Knock knock.
  Who's there?
Alaska.
  Alaska who?
**Alaska one more time to let
  me in!**

Knock knock.
  Who's there?
Yellow.
  Yellow who?
**Yellow, and how are you
  doing today?**

Knock knock.
  Who's there?
Handsome.
  Handsome who?
**Handsome food to me—I'm
  really hungry!**

Knock knock.
   Who's there?
Rabbit.
   Rabbit who?
**Rabbit carefully, it's a
   Christmas present!**

Knock knock.
   Who's there?
Sarah.
   Sarah who?
**Is Sarah doctor in the
   house? I feel sick!**

Knock knock.
   Who's there?
Ida.
   Ida who?
**Ida know, why don't you
   open up and find out?**

Knock knock.
   Who's there?
Oscar.
   Oscar who?
**Oscar a silly question, get a
   silly answer.**

Knock knock.
   Who's there?
Dishes.
   Dishes who?
**Dishes not the end of my
   knock knock jokes!**

Knock knock.
   Who's there?
Olive.
   Olive who?
**Olive these knock knock
   jokes are making me
   sick.**

Knock knock.
   Who's there?
Who.
   Who who?
**Are you an owl or
   something?**

Knock knock.
   Who's there?
Sombrero.
   Sombrero who?
Sombrero-ver the rainbow.

Knock knock.
 Who's there?
Ken.
 Ken who?
Ken you come out and play?

Knock knock.
 Who's there?
Itchy.
 Itchy who?
Bless you!

Knock knock.
 Who's there?
Ivan.
 Ivan who?
Ivan to come in, so please
 open the door!

Knock knock.
 Who's there?
Dwayne.
 Dwayne who?
Dwayne the bathtub! I'm
 drowning!

Knock knock.
 Who's there?
Walter.
 Walter who?
Walter you doing here so
 early?

Knock knock.
 Who's there?
Justin.
 Justin who?
You're Justin time for
 dinner.

Knock knock.
 Who's there?
Wanda.
 Wanda who?
Do you Wanda let me in yet?

Knock knock.
 Who's there?
Everest.
 Everest who?
Do we Everest from telling
 knock knock jokes?

Knock knock.
> Who's there?

Bill Gates.
> Bill Gates who?

Bill Gates a bike for his birthday.

Knock knock.
> Who's there?

Lion.
> Lion who?

Quit lion around and open the door.

Knock knock.
> Who's there?

Paws.
> Paws who?

Can you paws for a moment and open the door?

Knock knock.
> Who's there?

Zoo.
> Zoo who?

Zoo think you can come out and play?

Knock knock.
> Who's there?

Tide.
> Tide who?

Are you Tide of knock knock jokes yet?

Knock knock.
> Who's there?

Candace.
> Candace who?

Candace be the last knock knock joke?

Knock knock.
> Who's there?

Shirley.
> Shirley who?

Shirley I'll tell you another knock knock joke.

Knock knock.
> Who's there?

Aspen.
> Aspen who?

Aspen thinking about you all day.

Knock knock.
 Who's there?
Bonnie.
 Bonnie who?
It's Bonnie long time since
 I've seen you.

Knock knock.
 Who's there?
Andy.
 Andy who?
Andy-body want to go to the
 movies?

Knock knock.
 Who's there?
Isabel.
 Isabel who?
Isabel ringing or am I just
 hearing things?

Knock knock.
 Who's there?
Benjamin.
 Benjamin who?
I've Benjamin to the music
 all day.

Knock knock.
 Who's there?
Bailey.
 Bailey who?
I know you Bailey know me,
 but can I come in?

Knock knock.
 Who's there?
Byron.
 Byron who?
There's a Byron get one free
 sale at the mall!

Knock knock.
 Who's there?
Les.
 Les who?
Les one there is a rotten
 egg!

Knock knock.
 Who's there?
Baldwin.
 Baldwin who?
You'll be Baldwin you're
 older.

Knock knock.
Who's there?
Barry.
Barry who?
Let's Barry the hatchet and
be friends again.

Knock knock.
Who's there?
Carrie.
Carrie who?
Will you Carrie my books
for me?

Knock knock.
Who's there?
Calvin.
Calvin who?
Calvin you get there so I
know that you made it
safely.

Knock knock.
Who's there?
Colin.
Colin who?
Just Colin to tell you
another great knock
knock joke.

Knock knock.
Who's there?
Orange.
Orange who?
Orange you glad it's me?

Knock knock.
Who's there?
Conner.
Conner who?
Conner brother come out
and play?

Knock knock.
Who's there?
Jim.
Jim who?
Jim mind if I come in and
stay awhile?

Knock knock.
Who's there?
Mike.
Mike who?
Turn up the Mike so I can
hear you better.

Tongue Twisters

Try to Say These Ten Times Fast

Giggly gladiator.

Fresh French fries.

Selfish shellfish.

Sock, skirt, shirt.

Snatch stacked snacks.

Cheap cheese stinks.

Goofy gorillas gobble grapefruits.

Tall trees toss leaves.

Purple penguins pick pickles.

Cooked cookies crumble quickly.

Soggy stuff smells suspicious.

Big bad bears blow blue bubbles.

Tasty tomato tostadas.

You'll push she'll push.

Six slimy snails sailed silently.

Anonymous

A big black bug bit a big black dog
on his big black nose!

Kitty Morrow

Tongue Twisting Poems

Billy Button

Billy Button bought a buttered biscuit.
Did Billy Button buy a buttered biscuit?
If Billy Button bought a buttered biscuit,
Where's the buttered biscuit Billy Button bought?

Shirish Karker

A Fly and a Flea in a Flue

A fly and a flea in a flue
Were imprisoned, so what could they do?
Said the fly, "Let us flee!"
"Let us fly!" said the flea,
So they flew through a flaw in the flue.

Ogden Nash

Some Things to Think About

What do you call a male ladybug?

Why don't they call moustaches mouthbrows?

Why doesn't glue stick to the inside of the bottle?

What do they call their good plates in China?

Why is a boxing ring square?

If a fly didn't have wings, would we call it a walk?

Do fish ever get thirsty?

2

LAUGH -OUT- LOUD ANIMAL JOKES for KIDS

Q: Where do ants like to eat?

A: At a restaur-ant.

Q: What do alligators drink after they work out?

A: Gator-ade.

Q: What do a mouse and a wheel have in common?

A: They both squeak.

Q: What do frogs use so they can see better?

A: Frog-lights.

Q: Why can't you trust a pig?

A: It will always squeal on you.

Q: What kind of dog cries the most?

A: A Chi-wah-wah (Chihuahua).

Q: Where do birds invest their money?

A: In the stork market (stock market).

Q: Why can't you borrow money from a canary?

A: Because they're so cheep (cheap).

Q: What happened to the bee after he had four cups of coffee?

A: He got a buzz.

Q: Why was the bird nervous after lunch?

A: He had butterflies in his stomach.

Q: What did the father buffalo say to his son as he left for school?

A: "Bison (Bye, Son)."

Q: Where did the bat go to get some money?

A: The blood bank.

Q: What kind of bear doesn't have any teeth?

A: A gummy bear.

Q: What do you get from a pampered cow?

A: Spoiled milk.

Q: How did the cow make some extra money?

A: By mooooo-nlighting at another farm.

Q: Why did the cow become an astronaut?

A: So it could walk on the moooo-n.

Q: What do cows like to eat?

A: Smoooothies.

Did You Know . . .

- Cows give an average of 2,000 gallons of milk per year. That's over 30,000 glasses of milk!

  www.arsusda.gov

- There are about 11 million cows in America. They will make about 57.5 billion gallons of milk in a year.

  www.umpquadairy.com

Q: Why were the chickens so tired?

A: They were working around the cluck.

Q: What animals do you find in a monastery?

A: Chip-monks!

A duck walks into a store and asks the manager if he sells grapes. The manager says no, so the duck leaves. The next day the duck goes back to the store and asks the manager if he sells grapes. The manager says, "NO, we don't sell grapes," so the duck leaves the store. The next day the duck goes back to the same store and asks the manager if he sells grapes. The manager is furious now and says, "NO, WE DO NOT SELL GRAPES! IF YOU COME BACK AND ASK IF WE SELL GRAPES AGAIN, I'LL GLUE YOUR BEAK TO THE FLOOR!" The next day the duck goes back to the same store and says to the manager, "Excuse me, do you sell glue at this store?" The manager says, "No, we don't sell glue." The duck replies, "That's good. Do you sell grapes?"

Joe: **Did that dolphin splash you by accident?**

Bill: No, it was on porpoise!

Q: Where did the toy giraffe go when it was broken?

A: To get plastic surgery.

Q: What do you give a pig that has a cold?

A: Trough syrup!

Q: Why did the porcupine get sent home from the party?

A: He was popping all the balloons!

Q: What do you get when you cross a pig with a Christmas tree?

A: A pork-u-pine.

Q: What is a reptile's favorite movie?

A: The Lizard of Oz.

Q: Why did the snake lose his case in court?

A: He didn't have a leg to stand on.

Q: What kind of bull doesn't have horns?

A: A bullfrog.

Q: Why did the skunk have to stay in bed and take its medicine?

A: It was the doctor's odors.

Did You Know . . .

A shrimp's heart is located in its head.

Q: Why are fish so bad at basketball?

A: They don't like getting close to the net.

Q: Where do dogs go if they lose their tails?

A: The re-tail store.

Q: What are the funniest fish at the aquarium?

A: The clown fish.

Q: What is as big as an elephant but weighs zero pounds?

A: An elephant's shadow.

Q: Why are horses always so negative?

A: They say "neigh" (nay) to everything.

Q: What is black and white, black and white, black and white, black and white, splash?

A: A penguin rolling down an iceberg into the water.

Q: What is the smartest animal?

A: A snake, because no one can pull its leg.

Two men went deer hunting. One man asked the other, "Did you ever hunt bear?" The other hunter said, "No, but one time I went fishing in my shorts."

Q: Why did the robin go to the library?

A: It was looking for bookworms.

Q: What is black and white and red all over?

A: A penguin that's embarrassed.

Q: What do you call a pig that is no fun to be around?

A: A boar.

Q: What kind of fish can perform surgery?

A: Sturgeons.

Q: What do cats like to put in their milk?

A: Mice cubes.

Q: What do you get when you cross an elephant with a fish?

A: Swimming trunks.

Q: What do you do if your dog steals your spelling homework?

A: Take the words right out of his mouth.

Q: What did the whale say to the dolphin?

A: "Long time no sea (see)."

Q: What sound do porcupines make when they kiss?

A: Ouch!

Q: What happened when the frog's car broke down?

A: It had to be toad away (towed).

Q: What is a whale's favorite candy?

A: Blubber gum.

Q: What do you get when you cross a cow and a rabbit?

A: You get hare in your milk.

Q: Why did the horse keep falling over?

A: It just wasn't stable.

Q: How do fish pay their bills?

A: With sand-dollars.

Q: Which creatures on Noah's ark didn't come in pairs?

A: The worms—they came in apples.

Q: What kind of animal do you take into battle?

A: An army-dillo.

Did You Know . . .

Penguins can jump up to 6 feet high.

Q: What kind of bird likes to make bread?

A: The do-do bird (dough-dough).

Q: What do you get if you mix a rabbit and a snake?

A: A jump rope.

Q: How do you shoot a bumblebee?

A: With a bee-bee gun.

What Does the Bee Do?

What does the bee do?
Bring home honey.
And what does Father do?
Bring home money.
And what does Mother do?
Lay out the money.
And what does the baby do?
Eat up the honey.

Christina Rosetti

Q: Why do bumblebees smell so good?

A: They always wear bee-odorant.

Q: Why was the Tyrannosaurus rex so boring?

A: He was a dino-snore.

Q: What is a frog's favorite drink?

A: Croak-a-Cola.

Q: What is the scariest kind of bug?

A: A zom-bee (zombie).

Q: **Why are frogs so happy?**
A: They just eat whatever bugs them!

Q: **What is the difference between a fish and a piano?**
A: You can't tuna fish (tune a fish).

Q: **What did the horse say when he tripped and fell down?**
A: "Help! I've fallen and I can't giddy-up!"

Q: **If people like sandwiches, what do lions like?**
A: Man-wiches.

Q: **Why did the chicken cross the road?**
A: To show the squirrel it could be done.

Q: **Why did the turkey cross the road?**
A: To prove it wasn't a chicken.

Q: **What do you give a horse with a bad cold?**
A: Cough stirrup.

Q: **Who falls asleep at a bullfight?**
A: A bull-dozer.

Q: Why did the cat and her kittens clean up their mess?

A: They didn't want to litter.

Q: What is a sheep's favorite kind of food?

A: Bah-bah-cue.

Q: What is a hyena's favorite kind of candy?

A: A Snickers bar.

Q: How do sea creatures communicate under water?

A: With shell phones.

Q: Why was the dog depressed?

A: Because his life was so ruff.

Q: What does a rabbit use to fix its fur?

A: Hare-spray.

Q: What kind of insect is hard to understand?

A: A mumble-bee.

Q: What do you call a cow that can't give milk?

A: A milk dud.

Q: **Why did the chickens get in trouble at school?**

A: They were using fowl language.

Q: **Where does a lizard keep his groceries?**

A: In the refriger-gator.

Q: **Why is talking to cows a waste of time?**

A: Whatever you say goes in one ear and out the udder.

Q: **What do you get when you cross a dog with a cell phone?**

A: A golden receiver.

Q: **Where did the bull take the cow on a date?**

A: To dinner and a mooovie.

Q: **What is the world's hungriest animal?**

A: A turkey—it just gobble, gobble, gobbles!

Q: **What happened to the mouse when it fell in the bathtub?**

A: It came out squeaky clean.

Q: **Why did the cowboy ask his cattle so many questions?**

A: He wanted to grill them.

Q: **What is a duck's favorite snack?**
A: Cheese and quackers.

Q: **What do you call a cow that's afraid of everything?**
A: A cow-ard.

Q: **What is the difference between a cat and a frog?**
A: A cat has nine lives, but a frog croaks every day.

Q: **What does a frog say when he washes windows?**
A: "Rubbit, rubbit, rubbit."

Q: **What do you get when a lion escapes from the zoo?**
A: A cat-astrophe.

Q: **What is the best kind of cat to have around?**
A: A dandy-lion.

Q: **Where do trout keep their money?**
A: In a river bank.

Q: **What did the worm say to her daughter when she came home late?**
A: "Where on earth have you been?"

Q: What did the boy say when he threw a slug across the room?

A: "Man, how slime flies!"

Q: What do you get when you cross Bambi with an umbrella?

A: You get a rain-deer (reindeer).

Q: Who brings kittens for Christmas?

A: Santa Claws.

Q: What did Santa give Rudolph for his upset stomach?

A: Elk-A-Seltzer.

Q: Why can't an elephant's trunk be 12 inches long?

A: Because then it would be a a foot.

Q: What do you get when you cross a fish and a tree branch?

A: A fish stick.

Q: What kind of bird is always depressed?

A: A bluebird.

Q: How high can a bumblebee count?

A: To a buzz-illion.

Q: Why are oysters so strong?

A: Because of their mussels (muscles).

Q: What do you get when you throw a pony in the ocean?

A: A seahorse!

Q: What is the most colorful kind of snake in the world?

A: A rain-boa constrictor (rainbow).

Q: What does a cow keep in its wallet?

A: Moo-la.

Q: What kind of fish comes out at night?

A: A starfish.

Q: What did the dog say to its owner?

A: "I woof you."

Q: Why couldn't the dog visit the psychiatrist?

A: Because it wasn't allowed on the couch.

Q: What kind of cats like to play in the water?

A: Sea lions.

Knock knock!
    Who's there?
Moo.
    Moo, who?
Make up your mind—are you a cow or an owl?

Q: How does a dog say goodbye?

A: "Bone-Voyage!"

Q: What do llamas like to drink?

A: Strawberry llama-nade (lemonade).

Q: What do you call a fish with no eyes?

A: Fsh!

Q: What do you get when you throw a pig into the bushes?

A: A hedge-hog.

Q: What did the duck say to the clerk at the store?

A: "Just put it on my bill!"

Q: What did the frogs say to each other on their wedding day?

A: "I'll love you until the day I croak!"

Where Do Animals Come From?

Bees come from Stingapore
Cows come from Moo-rocco
Fish come from Wales
Sharks come from Finland
Ants come from Frants (France)
Dogs come from Bark-celona
   (Barcelona)
Pigs come from New Ham-shire
Chickens come from Turkey
Cats come from Purrr-u (Peru)
Birds come from Air-azona
Sheep come from the Baa-hamas
Snakes come from Hississippi

Q: Why was the golden retriever so stressed out?

A: Because he has so doggone much to do.

Q: Why was the horse in so much pain?

A: Because he was a charlie horse.

Q: What is red and weights 14,000 pounds?

A: An elephant holding its breath.

Q: What do cats like to eat for a snack?

A: Mice krispy bars.

Did You Know . . .

A hedgehog's heart beats 300 times per minute.

Q: How did the bunny rabbit feel when he ran out of carrots?

A: It made him unhoppy!

Q: What does a hen do when she goes grocery shopping?

A: She makes a list and chicks it twice!

Q: What did the fish say when it won the prize?

A: "That's fin-tastic (fantastic)!"

Q: Why did the grizzly tell the same story over and over?

A: Because he said it *bears* repeating!

Q: What will a moose do if he calls when you're not home?

A: He'll leave a detailed moose-age.

Q: What do you get when you put glasses on a pony?

A: A see-horse.

Q: Where to bunnies like to eat?

A: IHOP!

Q: How do you know when a rhino is ready to charge?

A: It gets out its credit card.

Knock knock!
 Who's there?
Raymond.
 Raymond who?
Raymond me to take the dog for a walk!

Q: **What do you call a racoon that crosses the road with his eyes shut?**

A: Roadkill!

Q: **Where should a 600-pound lion go?**

A: On a diet!

Q: **How do you keep a skunk from smelling?**

A: Hold its nose!

Did You Know . . .

A butterfly's tastebuds are in its feet.

Q: **What do you get when you cross a bear with a skunk?**

A: Winnie the Pew.

Q: **What kind of sea creature is always depressed?**

A: A blue whale.

Q: **What did the beaver say to the tree?**

A: "It's been nice getting to *gnaw* you! "

Q: What did the roach wear to the party?

A: A cockbroach.

Q: Why was the dog hungry all the time?

A: Because it was a chow.

Q: What kind of animal wears shoes while it's sleeping?

A: A horse!

Q: Why did the gum cross the road?

A: Because it was stuck to the chicken's shoe!

Q: How does a mother hen know when her chicks are ready to hatch?

A: She uses an egg timer.

Q: What happens when you get a thousand bunnies to line up and jump backwards?

A: You have a receding hare line!

Q: Where is the best place to park your dog?

A: The barking lot.

Q: What do you get when a cat climbs down your chimney with a bag of presents?

A: Santa Paws.

Q: Why can't you hear a dinosaur talk?

A: Because dinosaurs are extinct!

Q: Why don't lobsters share their toys?

A: Because they're shellfish (selfish)!

Knock knock!
> Who's there?

Either.
> Either who?

It's the Either Bunny!

Q: What is a chicken's favorite composer?

A: Bach, Bach, Bach!

Q: What is a fly's favorite composer?

A: Shoo-bert (Schubert).

Q: What do you get when you cross a bat and a cell phone?

A: A bat-mobile.

Q: Did you know that a kangaroo can jump higher than your house?

A: Of course! Your house can't jump!

Q: What time does a duck get up?

A: At the quack of dawn.

Q: What is black, white, and wet all over?

A: A zebra that was pushed into a swimming pool!

Q: What's black, white, and laughing?

A: The zebra that pushed the other zebra into the swimming pool!

Q: Why don't bunnies tell scary stories?

A: Because it makes the hare stand up on the back of their necks.

Q: What do you call a man with a seagull on his head?
A: Cliff.

Q: What do you call a monkey in a minefield?
A: A ba-BOOM!

Q: What do you call a pig that took a plane?
A: Swine flew (flu).

Q: What was the elephant doing on the freeway?
A: I don't know—about 10 miles per hour?

Jack: Do you like that cow over there?

Jill: No, I like the udder one!

Q: What do cats use to do their homework?

A: A meow-culator.

Did You Know . . .

The chow is the only dog that does not have a pink tongue.

Q: Why did the hornet have to fly back home?

A: Because he forgot his yellow jacket.

Q: Why did the bee visit the barber?

A: Because he wanted a buzz cut.

Bill: Would you like some honey?

Bob: May-bee!

Q: How did the bee get ready for school?

A: She used her honey comb!

Q: What do you get when you cross a vulture and a bumblebee?

A: A buzz-ard.

Q: What is a horse's favorite kind of fruit?

A: Straw-berries.

Q: What is a horse's favorite kind of nut?

A: Hay-zelnuts.

Q: What is a mouse's favorite game?

A: Hide and squeak.

Q: Why do birds fly south for the winter?

A: Because it's too far to walk, and their feet won't reach the pedals on a bicycle!

Cow #1: Did you hear about that crazy disease going around called mad cow disease?

Cow #2: I sure did—good thing I'm a penguin!

A policeman saw a lady with a hippopotamus walking down the street. He said, "Ma'am, you need to take that hippo to the zoo." The next day the lady was again walking down the street with the hippopotamus. The policeman said, "Ma'am, I told you to take that hippo to the zoo." The lady replied, "I did take him to the zoo, and today I'm taking him to the movies!"

Q: What is the best way to communicate with a squirrel?

A: Climb up a tree and act like a nut!

Q: Why can't cats drink milk in outer space?

A: Because the milk is in flying saucers!

Q: What's more annoying than a cat meowing outside your bedroom window?

A: *Ten* cats meowing outside your bedroom window!

Q: What do you do when you come upon two snails fighting?

A: Just let them slug it out . . .

Did You Know . . .

An ostrich's eye is bigger than its brain.

Q: What's the best way to learn about spiders?

A: On a web-site!

Q: What does a frog drink when it wants to lose weight?

A: Diet Croak.

Q: Why did the firefly get bad grades on his report card?

A: Because he wasn't very bright!

Q: Why was the caterpillar running for its life?

A: Because it was being chased by a dog-erpillar!

The Caterpillar

Caterpillar
Brown and furry
Caterpillar in a hurry,
Take a walk
To the shady lead, or stalk,
Or what not,
Which may be the chosen spot.
No toad spy you,
Hovering bird of prey pass by you;
Spin and die,
To live again a butterfly.

Christina Rosetti

Q: What do you get when you cross a dog and a snowman?

A: Frostbite.

Q: What is the difference between a fly and an eagle?

A: An eagle can fly, but a fly can't eagle.

Did You Know . . .

The golden poison dart frog is one of the most poisonous animals on earth. A single two-inch frog has enough venom to kill ten grown men

www.nationalgeographic.com

Q: **When is it bad luck to see a black cat?**

A: When you're a mouse!

A duck went shopping at the grocery story and went to the register to pay. The store clerk asked, "Don't you have exact change?" The duck answered, "Nope, sorry, I only carry bills!"

Q: **What do you call an elephant that never takes a bath?**

A: A smell-ephant!

Q: **What is a fish's favorite game show?**

A: Name that tuna (tune).

Knock knock!
    Who's there?
Bee.
    Bee who?
Just bee yourself!

Knock knock!
  Who's there?
Owl.
  Owl who?
Owl tell you another joke if you let me in . . .

Knock knock!
  Who's there?
Aardvark.
  Aardvark who?
Aardvark a thousand miles just to see you!

Knock knock!
  Who's there?
Amos.
  Amos who?
Ouch! Amos-quito bit me!

Knock knock!
  Who's there?
Bug spray.
  Bug spray who?
Bug spray they won't get squished!

Q: Where do horses live?

A: In neigh-borhoods.

Q: What kind of fish are worth a lot of money?

A: Goldfish.

Q: Where do monkeys make their burgers?

A: On the grill-a (gorilla).

Q: What did one nightcrawler say to the other nightcrawler?

A: "I know this great place down the road where we can eat dirt cheap! "

Q: Why does a herd of deer have plenty of money?

A: Because they have a lot of bucks!

Did You Know . . .

An owl can't move its eyeballs.

Q: What is a bug's favorite music?

A: The Beatles.

Q: What is a frogs favorite outdoor game?

A: Croak-quet (croquet).

Q: What kind of animal will never leave you alone?

A: The badger.

Q: Why did the bug get up early every morning?

A: Because it was a praying mantis.

Q: What kind of animal always contradicts itself?

A: A hippo-crite.

Q: Where do you put your dog when he's not behaving?

A: In the grrrrrage!

Q: What do you call a cat with eight legs that can swim?

A: An octo-puss.

Q: Why were the robins eating cake?

A: Because it was their bird-thday!

Q: Why did the pythons decide to get married?

A: Because they had a crush on each other.

Q: What do you do if there is a lion in your bed?

A: Go to a hotel for the night!

Q: What do you get when you cross a snail and a porcupine?

A: A slow poke.

Q: What's green, has six legs, and climbs bean stalks?

A: The Jolly Green Gi-ant.

Q: What's grey and goes round and round and round?

A: An elephant on a merry-go-round.

Q: Why did the racoon cross the road twice?

A: Because it was a double crosser.

Q: What do you get when you have a bunch of giraffes on the highway?

A: A giraffic jam.

Q: What performs at the circus and flies around eating mosquitos?

A: An acro-bat.

Q: Why was the crow on the phone?

A: Because he was making a long distance phone caw!

Customer: Do you serve turkeys here?

Waitress: We serve anyone, so go ahead and take a seat.

Q: How do fleas travel from dog to dog?

A: By *itch* hiking.

Knock knock!
   Who's there?
Gnat.
   Gnat who?
I'm *gnat* who you think I am!

Knock knock!
   Who's there?
Moose.
   Moose who? .
It *moose* be time to let me in, so open the door!

Q: **How do you know which end of a worm is the head?**
A: Tickle the middle and see which end laughs.

Q: **Why are chickens so bad at baseball?**
A: Because they're always hitting fowl balls.

Q: **What do you get when you cross a beetle and a rabbit?**
A: Bugs bunny!

Q: **What do skunks like to eat when they're hungry?**
A: Peanut butter and smelly sandwiches.

Q: **What do you get when you cross a penguin and a jalapeño?**
A: A chilly pepper.

Q: Why can't you trust what a pig says?

A: Because it's full of bologna.

Q: What's large, gray, and has eighteen wheels?

A: An elephant in a semi-truck.

Q: What is a polar bear's favorite breakfast?

A: Ice krispies.

Q: Why did all the animals fall asleep in the barn?

A: Because the pigs were so boar-ing (boring).

Q: Why didn't the snake know how much it weighed?

A: Because it shed its scales.

Q: What does a leopard say after dinner?

A: "That hit the spot!"

Did You Know . . .

A bat lives about 40 years.

Q: How does a cow get to church on Sunday?

A: On its moo-tercycle.

Q: Why did the moose lift weights at the gym?

A: Because it wanted big moose-les (muscles).

Q: Why didn't the crab spend any of his money?

A: Because he was a penny pincher.

Q: What does a cow like to drink before bed?

A: De-calf-inated coffee (decaffeinated).

Q: What are you doing if you're staring at a starfish?

A: Stargazing.

Q: Why was the duck happy after his doctor appointment?

A: Because he got a clean bill of health.

Q: Where do bugs go to do their shopping?

A: The flea market.

Q: What kind of dessert do dogs run away from?

A: Pound cake.

Q: How do you know if there is a black bear in your oven?

A: The oven door won't close!

Q: Why did the cheetah get glasses?

A: Because it was seeing spots.

Knock knock!
    Who's there?
Cod.
    Cod who?
Cod **you let me in? It's cold out here!**

Knock knock!
    Who's there?
Shellfish.
    Shellfish who?
Don't be shellfish—let me in!

Knock knock!
    Who's there?
Rhino.
    Rhino who?
Rhino you want to let me in.

Knock knock!
    Who's there?
Raven.
    Raven who?
I've been *raven* about you to all my friends, so won't you let me in?

Q: What is the richest bird in the world?

A: The golden eagle.

Q: Why was a pig on the airplane?

A: Because its owner wanted to see pigs fly.

Q: Why was the frog in a bad mood?

A: Because he was having a toad-ally bad day.

Q: What do you call an elephant in a phone booth?

A: Stuck!

Q: Why were the elephants kicked off the beach?

A: Because they kept throwing their trunks in the water.

Q: Where do old ants go?

A: The ant-ique store.

Q: What do you get when you cross a cow and a toad?

A: A bullfrog.

Q: What do you get when you cross a water buffalo and a chicken?

A: Soggy buffalo wings.

Q: How do chickens stay in shape?

A: They eggs-ercise.

Q: How do skunks watch the news?

A: On their smellevision.

Q: Why did the rabbit work at the hotel?

A: Because he made a good bellhop.

Josh: How do you know carrots are good for your eyes?

Anna: Have you ever seen a rabbit wearing glasses?

Q: What do dinosaurs put in their cars?

A: Fossil fuel.

Q: How did the pig write a letter?

A: With its pig pen.

Did You Know . . .

An ant can lift 20 times its own body weight.

What's Their Motto?

Bee: Mind your own beeswax.

Bear: Grin and bear it.

Cow: Keep moooooving.

Dog: Don't bark up the wrong tree.

Owl: It's not what you know, it's WHO you know.

Rabbit: Don't worry, be hoppy.

Cat: Don't litter.

Mouse: The squeaky wheel gets the grease.

Bat: Just *fang* in there.

Otter: Do unto *otters* as you would have them do unto you.

Robin: The early bird gets the worm.

Fox: Don't count your chickens before they're hatched.

Fish: Absence makes the heart grow flounder.

Q: **What happened to the snake when it got upset?**

A: It got hiss-terical.

Q: **What did the rattlesnakes do after they had a fight?**

A: They hissed and made up.

Did You Know . . .

The king cobra can grow to over 18 feet long. It's the largest poisonous snake in the world. Just a small amount of its venom can kill up to 30 people.

Q: **What does a monkey drink with its breakfast?**

A: Ape juice.

Q: **What happened to the platypus when it fell in the hole?**

A: It became a *splaty*pus.

Q: **How do crocodiles make their dinner?**

A: In a croc pot.

Q: Where do ants go when it's hot outside?
A: Ant-arctica.

Q: Why do pigs make great comedians?
A: Because they like to ham it up.

Q: What is a pig's favorite play?
A: Hamlet.

Q: Where do pigs put their dirty laundry?
A: In the hamper.

Q: Why was the pig having trouble walking?
A: Because he pulled his hamstring.

Q: What do you get if you cross a dog and a mosquito?
A: A bloodhound.

Did You Know . . .

The duckbill platypus can store over 500 worms in its cheeks.

Q: What do you get when you combine a cat and a dog?

A: Cat nip.

Q: What does a squirrel like to eat for breakfast?

A: Dough-nuts!

Q: What is a monkey's favorite book?

A: Apes of Wrath.

Q: How do skunks get in touch with each other?

A: They use their smell phones.

Q: How do crabs call each other?

A: They use their shell phones.

Q: What do you call a ladybug that won't clean up its room?

A: A litter bug.

Knock knock!
Who's there?
Otter.
Otter who?
You otter open this door and let me in!

Knock knock!
　Who's there?
Dragon.
　Dragon who?
Quit dragon this out and open the door!

Q: What happened to the rich snake who had everything?

A: He decided to scale back.

Q: How do you stop a 10-pound parrot from talking too much?

A: Buy a 20-pound cat?

Q: Why did the cat study its spelling words fifty times?

A: Because practice makes purr-fect.

At The Zoo

First I saw the white bear, then I saw the black;
Then I saw the camel with a hump upon his back;
Then I saw the grey wolf, with mutton in his maw;
Then I saw the wombat waddle in the straw;
Then I saw the elephant a-waving of his trunk;
Then I saw the monkeys—mercy, how unpleasantly
　they smelt!

William Makepeace Thackeray

Q: What do you get when you cross a brontosaurus and a lemon?

A: A dino-sour.

Q: What's green, has warts, and lives alone?

A: Hermit the frog.

Q: Why was the bird wearing a wig?

A: Because it was a bald eagle.

Q: What did the baby shark do when it got lost in the ocean?

A: It whaled (wailed).

Q: What kind of house does a pig live in?

A: A hog cabin.

Q: How do frogs send a telegraph?

A: They use Morse toad (code).

Q: How did the frog get over the tall wall?

A: With a tad-pole.

Q: What is a cow's favorite vegetable?

A: Cow-iflower.

Q: Why did the pigs write a lot of letters?

A: Because they were pen pals.

Q: What does a cat wear at night?

A: Its paw-jamas.

Q: What did the night crawler's parents say after their child got home after curfew?

A: "Where on earth have you been?"

"Ode to a Cricket"

Little cricket is up at dawn
Getting dressed, has one shoe on
Little Annie Dachshund came out to play
And she spied Mr. Cricket right away!
Run cricket run
Annie will get you
Cricket ran, cricket flew
Cricket lost his little shoe
Doesn't matter, come what may
Annie got him anyway!

Virginia Satterfield Totsch

Q: Where did the fish go each morning?

A: To their school.

Q: What does a racehorse like to eat for lunch?

A: Fast food.

Q: What do you give a mouse on its birthday?

A: Cheese-cake.

Knock knock!
  Who's there?
Iguana.
  Iguana who?
Iguana come in, so please open up!

Emma: If Noah got milk from the cows, eggs from the chickens, and wool from the sheep on the ark, what did he get from the ducks?

Leah: I don't know, Emma, what?

Emma: Quackers!

Q: Which animal on the ark had the highest IQ?

A: The giraffe!

Q: What do you get when you pour boiling water down a rabbit hole?

A: Hot Cross Bunnies.

Knock knock!
  Who's there?
Owl.
  Owl who?
I'm tired of knocking, so *owl* see you later.

Q: What do cobras put on their bathroom floor?
A: Rep-tiles.

Q: What's a cow's favorite painting?
A: The Moo-na Lisa.

Q: What is a bee's favorite toy?
A: A fris-bee!

Q: What is a dolphin's favorite game show?
A: Whale of Fortune.

Q: What does a goat use when it's camping?
A: A sheeping bag.

Q: What kind of dog is good at chemistry?
A: A Lab-rador retriever.

Q: What is a lightning bug's favorite game?
A: Hide and glow seek.

Q: Why did the cat go to the beauty salon?
A: It needed a pet-icure.

Q: **How did the leopard lose its spots?**

A: It took a bath and came out spotless.

Q: **What did the firefly say before the big race?**

A: "Ready, set, glow!"

Did You Know . . .

The tongue of a blue whale can weigh as much as a full-grown elephant.

Q: **What did the firefly have for lunch?**

A: A light meal.

Q: **What did the wolf say when it met its new neighbors?**

A: "Howl are you doing?"

Q: **Why don't goats mind their own business?**

A: Because they're always butting in.

Q: **What did the mother possum say to her son?**

A: "Quit hanging around all day and do something!"

Q: Why did the cat vanish into thin air?

A: Because it drank evaporated milk.

Q: Where do cows go to dance?

A: The meatball.

Knock knock!
   Who's there?
Seal.
   Seal who?
My lips are sealed until you open the door!

Q: What lives in a hole, has horns, and runs really fast?

A: An ant-elope.

Q: What kind of tree has the most bark?

A: The dogwood tree.

Q: Why didn't the bug feel like doing anything?

A: Because it was a slug.

Q: What's a bird's favorite movie?

A: Batman and Robin.

Q: What happened to the worm when it didn't clean its room?

A: It was grounded.

Q: Why did the cat have trouble using its computer?

A: Because it kept eating the mouse.

Q: Why did the mosquito wake up in the middle of the night?

A: It was having a bite-mare.

Knock knock!
Who's there?
Goat.
Goat who?
You're getting my goat—just let me in!

Q: What is a wolf's favorite treat?

A: Pigs in a blanket.

Q: What is a wolf's favorite book?

A: Little Howl on the Prairie.

Q: What did the bird wear to the ball?

A: A duck-sedo (tuxedo).

Q: **Why did the dinosaur cross the road?**

A: To eat the chickens on the other side.

Q: **When can an elephant sit under an umbrella and not get wet?**

A: When it's not raining.

Q: **What is the sleepiest dinosaur?**

A: The Bronto-snore-ous.

Q: **What do you get when a rhinoceros goes running through your garden?**

A: Squash.

Q: **Why did the dog quit playing football?**

A: The game got too ruff (rough).

Q: **What do you get when you cross a pig and a cow?**

A: A ham-burger.

Q: **What do you do if a cow won't give milk?**

A: You mooove on to the udder one.

Q: **Why did the horse wake up in the middle of the night?**

A: It was having a night-mare.

Q: What do you get when a pig does karate?

A: Pork chops!

Q: Where do cats shop for their toys?

A: From a toy cat-alog.

Q: How are A's just like flowers?

A: Bees follow them.

Q: Where do fish like to sleep?

A: On their water beds.

Q: What kind of birds like to stick together?

A: Vel-crows.

Q: What do you get when you cross a salmon and an elephant?

A: Swim trunks.

Q: What is a frog's favorite snack?

A: French flies.

Q: What is big, gray, and wears glass slippers?

A: Cinderelephant.

Q: Why do fish make good lawyers?

A: Because they like de-bait.

Q: What do you get when a barn full of cows won't give milk?

A: Udder chaos.

Q: What do you call it when one cow is spying on another cow?

A: A steak out.

Tim: My dog keeps chasing people on a bike!

Tom: Why don't you put him on a leash?

Tim: No, I think I'll just take his bike away.

Q: What's a cow's favorite game?

A: Moo-sical chairs.

Q: What kind of keys never unlock anything?

A: Monkeys, turkeys, and donkeys.

Jill: How do elephants smell?

Jane: Not very good!

Q: What has two heads, four eyes, six legs, and a tail?

A: A cowboy on a horse.

Q: Where do bears keep their clothes?
A: In a claw-set (closet).

Q: What kind of bugs wear sneakers?
A: Shoo flies (shoe flies).

Q: What game do leopards always lose?
A: Hide and seek—they always get spotted.

Q: Why are snails shy at parties?
A: They don't want to come out of their shell.

Q: Why did the bull owe so much money?
A: Because it always charged.

Q: What is a chicken's favorite game?
A: Duck, duck, goose.

Q: Did you hear about the dog that didn't have any teeth?
A: Its bark was worse than its bite.

Q: What do dogs have that no other animals have?
A: Puppies.

Knock knock!
Who's there?
Fur.
Fur who?
I'm waiting fur you to open the door!

Q: What has a horn but does not honk?
A: A rhinoceros.

Q: Why do dragons sleep all day?
A: Because they like to hunt knights.

Q: What kind of bone is hard for a dog to eat?
A: A trombone.

Q: How did the gorilla fix its bike?
A: With a monkey wrench.

Q: What is a woodpecker's favorite kind of joke?
A: A knock-knock joke.

Q: What do you call a story about a giraffe?
A: A tall tale.

Q: What did the vet give to the sick parakeet?
A: A special tweetment.

Anna: Can a seagull eat fifty fish in an hour?

Leah: No, but a peli-can!

Q: What kind of bee is good for your health?

A: Vitamin B.

Did you know . . .

There are only two types of egg-laying mammals: the duck-billed platypus and the echidna (also known as the spiny anteater). Both are only found in Australia and New Guinea.

Q: What do you get when you put a pig in a blender?

A: Bacon bits.

Q: Why do elephants have trunks?

A: Because they would look silly with suitcases.

Q: What kind of dogs can tell time?

A: Watch dogs.

Q: What do you get when you combine a bear and a pig?

A: A teddy boar.

Q: **How did the bird open the can of birdseed?**

A: With a crow-bar.

Two cockroaches are eating together in a garbage can. One cockroach says to the other, "Did you hear about the new restaurant that opened up down the road? It has the cleanest kitchen I've ever seen. The place sparkles and shines. There isn't a crumb anywhere to be found!" The other cockroach looked up and said, "Please stop! I'm eating here!"

Q: **What do woodpeckers eat for breakfast?**

A: Oakmeal.

Q: **How do dolphins make hard decisions?**

A: By flippering a coin.

Q: **Why was the lion always tired?**

A: It would only take cat naps.

Q: **What is the smartest bird in the world?**

A: Owl-bert Einstein.

Q: **What kind of animal never gets old?**

A: A gnu (new).

Q: How do turkeys travel across the ocean?

A: In a gravy boat.

Q: What did the wolf do when he heard the joke?

A: He howled.

Q: What did the spider say to the fly?

A: "Why don't you stick around for a while?"

Q: How do you grow a blackbird?

A: Plant some bird seed.

Q: Why did the turkey have a stomachache?

A: He gobbled up his food too fast.

Knock knock!
   Who's there?
Bat.
   Bat who?
I bat you're going to let me in soon!

Did You Know . . .

A gnu is another name for a wildebeest.

Q: What did the mouse say when he lost his piece of cheese?

A: Rats!

Q: What is a cat's favorite dessert?

A: Mice cream.

Did You Know . . .

Benjamin Franklin wanted our nation's bird to be a wild turkey instead of the bald eagle.

Q: Where do skunks like to sit in church?

A: In the front pew.

Josh: Should I go see the prairie dogs in Texas?

Anna: Sure Josh, gopher it!

Q: What do you get when you cross a deer and a pirate?

A: A buck-aneer.

Q: Why was the elephant mad at the bellman?

A: He dropped its trunk.

Q: What happened when the giraffes had a race?

A: They were neck and neck the whole time.

Q: Why didn't the llama get any dessert?

A: He wouldn't eat his llama beans (lima beans).

Q: What does a cat do when he wants popcorn in the middle of the movie?

A: He pushes the paws button.

Knock knock!
  Who's there?
Elephant.
  Elephant who?
You forgot to feed the elephant?!

Knock knock!
  Who's there?
Badger.
  Badger who?
I'll stop *badger*ing you if you let me in!

Q: What do polar bears eat for lunch?
A: Iceberg-ers.

Q: How can you tell if a moose has been in your freezer?
A: By the moose tracks.

Q: What did one cat say to the other cat?
A: "Can you hear me meow?"

Knock knock!
   Who's there?
Lion.
   Lion who?
Quit lion around and answer the door already!

Patient: Doctor, I have a problem. I think I'm a moth.

Doctor: I don't think you should be seeing me. I think you need a psychiatrist!

Patient: I know, but I was on my way there and I saw you had your light on.

Patient: Doctor, I think I'm a chicken.

Doctor: How long have you been feeling this way?

Patient: Ever since I was a little egg.

Did You Know . . .

The average hen lays 19 dozen eggs in a year.

Silly Animal Tongue Twisters

(Say these three times as fast as you can!)

Kitty catty, paws, claws, mouse, house, whiskers, tricksters, fur, purr, pounce!

Purple penguins play ping pong.

Bullfrogs blow big bubbles.

Sneaky snakes slither slowly.

Big bears bounce balls.

Skinks think skunks stink.

Beefy blazing bison burgers.

Moths thought sloths got flaws.

3

KNOCK-KNOCK JOKES for KIDS

Knock knock.
    Who's there?
Amanda.
    Amanda who?
**Amanda fix the plumbing is
    here.**

Knock knock.
    Who's there?
Billy Bob Joe Penny.
    Billy Bob Joe Penny who?
**Seriously, how many Billy
    Bob Joe Penny's do you
    know?**

Knock knock.
    Who's there?
Weirdo.
    Weirdo who?
**Weirdo you think you're
    going?**

Knock knock.
    Who's there?
Leah.
    Leah who?
**Leah the door unlocked
    next time!**

Knock knock.
    Who's there?
Alden.
    Alden who?
**When you're Alden with
    your dinner, can you
    come out and play?**

Knock knock.
    Who's there?
Avery.
    Avery who?
**Avery nice person is
    knocking on the door.
    You should come take a
    look.**

Knock knock.
    Who's there?
Lena.
    Lena who?
Lena little closer and I'll tell
    you another joke.

Knock knock.
    Who's there?
Nick.
    Nick who?
You're just in the Nick of
    time. I was getting ready
    to tell another knock-
    knock joke!

Knock knock.
    Who's there?
West.
    West who?
Let me know if you need a
    west from these knock-
    knock jokes.

Knock knock.
    Who's there?
Leon.
    Leon who?
Leon me when you're not
    strong.

Knock knock.
    Who's there?
Ash.
    Ash who?
It sounds like you're
    catching a cold.

Knock knock.
    Who's there?
Mustache.
    Mustache who?
I mustache you a question,
    so let me in!

Knock knock.
    Who's there?
Jimmy.
    Jimmy who?
If you Jimmy a key, I'll let
    myself in.

Knock knock.
> Who's there?

Will.
> Will who?

Will you listen to another knock-knock joke?

Knock knock.
> Who's there?

Erin.
> Erin who?

I have to run a quick Erin, but I'll be back!

Knock knock.
> Who's there?

Eddy.
> Eddy who?

Eddy-body home?

Knock knock.
> Who's there?

Oliver.
> Oliver who?

Oliver doors are locked, let me in!

Knock knock.
> Who's there?

Alice.
> Alice who?

Well, you know what they say; Alice fair in love and war.

Knock knock.
> Who's there?

Wendy.
> Wendy who?

Wendy wind blows de cradle will rock.

Knock knock.
> Who's there?

Wayne.
> Wayne who?

Wayne drops are falling on my head, can you let me in?

Knock knock.
> Who's there?

Max.
> Max who?

Max no difference to me.

Knock knock.
   Who's there?
Toby.
   Toby who?
Toby or not Toby; that is
   the question, and you'll
   have to open up to find
   out!

Knock knock.
   Who's there?
France.
   France who?
France stick closer than a
   brother.

Knock knock.
   Who's there?
Peas.
   Peas who?
Peas tell me some more
   knock-knock jokes.

Knock knock.
   Who's there?
Gwen.
   Gwen who?
Gwen do you think you can
   come out and play?

Knock knock.
   Who's there?
Watson.
   Watson who?
Watson the radio?

Knock knock.
   Who's there?
Wok.
   Wok who?
I wok all the way here, and
   you won't even let me
   come in!

Knock knock.
   Who's there?
Yeast.
   Yeast who?
You could at yeast come to
   the door and say hi!

Knock knock.
   Who's there?
Collie.
   Collie who?
Collie-flower is good for
   you.

Knock knock.
Who's there?
Sofa.
Sofa who?
Sofa these have been good knock-knock jokes.

Knock knock
Who's there?
Window.
Window who?
Window I get to hear some more knock-knock jokes?

Knock knock.
Who's there?
Cheese.
Cheese who?
For cheese a jolly good fellow, for cheese a jolly good fellow.

Knock knock.
Who's there?
Boil.
Boil who?
Boil you like this next joke!

Knock knock.
Who's there?
Mushroom.
Mushroom who?
There's mushroom for improvement on that last joke.

Knock knock.
Who's there?
Pizza.
Pizza who?
I'm going to give him a pizza my mind!

Knock knock.
Who's there?
Pesto.
Pesto who?
I hate to make a pesto myself, but I'm going to keep knocking until you open.

Knock knock.
>Who's there?

Gluten.
>Gluten who?

You're going to be a gluten for punishment if you don't open up!

Knock knock.
>Who's there?

Shellfish.
>Shellfish who?

Don't be shellfish, open up and share!

Knock knock.
>Who's there?

Darleen.
>Darleen who?

Please be a Darleen and open the door for me.

Knock knock.
>Who's there?

Les.
>Les who?

Les tell some more knock-knock jokes!

Knock knock.
>Who's there?

Gino.
>Gino who?

Gino, these knock-knock jokes are kind of fun.

Knock knock.
>Who's there?

Gladys.
>Gladys who?

I'm Gladys time for another knock-knock joke.

Knock knock.
>Who's there?

Otto.
>Otto who?

You really Otto open the door.

Knock knock
>Who's there?

Earl.
>Earl who?

Earl to bed, Earl to rise.

Knock knock.
Who's there?
Jewel.
Jewel who?
Jewel have to let me in soon.

Knock knock
Who's there?
Hobbit.
Hobbit who?
Sorry, telling knock-knock
jokes is a bad hobbit I'm
trying to break.

Knock knock.
Who's there?
Dee.
Dee who?
Dee cake is in Dee oven.

Knock knock.
Who's there?
Ben Hur.
Ben Hur who?
Ben Hur for a while now,
can you let me in?

Knock knock.
Who's there?
Rupert.
Rupert who?
Rupert your left foot in,
Rupert your left foot
out.

Knock knock.
Who's there?
Radio.
Radio who?
Radio or not, here I come!

Knock knock.
Who's there?
Allison.
Allison who?
Allison for someone to
come to the door, but
I don't hear anybody
coming.

Knock knock.
　Who's there?
Sandy.
　Sandy who?
**Open up and let's go to the
　Sandy beaches.**

Knock knock.
　Who's there?
Penny.
　Penny who?
Penny for your thoughts?

Knock knock.
　Who's there?
Mickey.
　Mickey who?
**Mickey won't fit in the
　keyhole, can you let me
　in?**

Emma:	**Will you remember me in an hour?**
Anna:	Yes.
Emma:	**Will you remember me in a day?**
Anna:	Yes.
Emma:	**Will you remember me in a week?**
Anna:	Yes.
Emma:	**Will you remember me in a month?**
Anna:	Yes.
Emma:	**Will you remember me in a year?**
Anna:	Yes.
Emma:	**I don't think you will.**
Anna:	Sure I will!
Emma:	**Knock knock.**
Anna:	Who's there?
Emma:	**See, you forgot me already!**

Knock knock.
  Who's there?
Yule.
  Yule who?
**Yule never know who it is
  unless you open the
  door!**

Knock knock.
  Who's there?
Benjamin.
  Benjamin who?
**I've Benjamin on my guitar
  all day!**

Knock knock.
  Who's there?
Ear.
  Ear who?
**Ear is another knock-knock
  joke—are you ready?**

Knock knock.
  Who's there?
Waddle.
  Waddle who?
**Waddle you do if I tell
  another knock-knock
  joke?**

Knock knock.
  Who's there?
Howl.
  Howl who?
**Howl I open the door if it's
  locked?**

Knock knock.
  Who's there?
Uno.
  Uno who?
Uno who this is?

Knock knock.
  Who's there?
Scott.
  Scott who?
**There's Scott to be better a
  better knock-knock joke
  than this one!**

Knock knock.
  Who's there?
Wanda.
  Wanda who?
Wanda come out and play?

Knock knock.
 Who's there?
Nobel.
 Nobel who?
There was Nobel so I had to knock!

Knock knock.
 Who's there?
Mabel.
 Mabel who?
Mabel isn't working right either.

Knock knock.
 Who's there?
Leaf.
 Leaf who?
I'm not going to leaf so you had better let me in!

Knock knock.
 Who's there?
Figs.
 Figs who?
Figs your doorbell, it's not working!

Knock knock.
 Who's there?
Butter.
 Butter who?
Butter open up—it looks like rain out here!

Knock knock.
 Who's there?
Udder.
 Udder who?
Would you like to hear an udder knock-knock joke?

Knock knock.
 Who's there?
Claws.
 Claws who?
Claws the window—it's cold in here!

Knock knock.
 Who's there?
Auntie.
 Auntie who?
Auntie going to let me in yet?

Knock knock.
Who's there?
Irish.
Irish who?
Irish you would open the
door now!

Knock knock.
Who's there?
Rita.
Rita who?
Rita good book lately?

Knock knock.
Who's there?
Watson.
Watson who?
Can you tell me Watson
your mind?

Knock knock.
Who's there?
Annie.
Annie who?
Annie thing you can do I
can do better.

Knock knock.
Who's there?
Annie.
Annie who?
Annie chance you want to
hear another knock-
knock joke?

Knock knock.
Who's there?
Myth.
Myth who?
I myth seeing you!

Knock knock.
Who's there?
Jacob.
Jacob who?
Jacob your mind! Do you
want to hear another
knock-knock joke?

Knock knock.
Who's there?
Stu.
Stu who?
It's Stu late to ask any
questions!

Knock knock.
Who's there?
Justin.
Justin who?
I think I got here Justin time!

Knock knock.
Who's there?
Adolf.
Adolf who?
Adolf ball hit me on the mouth, and my lip swelled up.

Knock knock.
Who's there?
Lionel.
Lionel who?
Lionel always get you in trouble, so tell the truth!

Knock knock.
Who's there?
Manny.
Manny who?
How Manny knock-knock jokes do you want to hear?

Knock knock.
Who's there?
Dawn.
Dawn who?
Please Dawn leave me out here in the rain.

Knock knock.
Who's there?
Adore.
Adore who?
Adore is between you and me, so please open up!

Knock knock.
Who's there?
Eamon.
Eamon who?
Eamon the mood for some more knock-knock jokes, how about you?

Knock knock.
Who's there?
Quiche.
Quiche who?
Can I have a hug and a quiche?

Knock knock.
  Who's there?
Countess.
  Countess who?
Does this countess a funny
  knock-knock joke?

Knock knock.
  Who's there?
Kenya.
  Kenya who?
Kenya open the door,
  please?

Knock knock.
  Who's there?
Owen.
  Owen who?
I'm Owen you some money,
  so open up and I'll pay
  you back.

Knock knock.
  Who's there?
Les.
  Les who?
Open the door and Les be
  friends!

Knock knock.
  Who's there?
Norway.
  Norway who?
There is Norway I'm going
  to just stand here, so
  open the door!

Knock knock.
  Who's there?
Nacho cheese.
  Nacho cheese who?
That is nacho cheese, so give
  it back!

Knock knock.
  Who's there?
You.
  You who?
You-hoo, it's me, can I come
  in?

Knock knock.
  Who's there?
Betty.
  Betty who?
I Betty doesn't know who
  this is!

Knock knock.
Who's there?
Robin.
Robin who?
No, Robin Hood. He steals from the rich and gives to the poor.

Knock knock.
Who's there?
Misty.
Misty who?
I misty chance to see you— will you let me come in?

Knock knock.
Who's there?
Summer.
Summer who?
Summer these jokes are funny, but some aren't!

Knock knock.
Who's there?
Sharon.
Sharon who?
I'm Sharon my cookies if you'll let me in!

Knock knock.
Who's there?
Hayden.
Hayden who?
Come out and play Hayden go seek!

Knock knock
Who's there?
Asaid.
Asaid who?
Asaid open the door, it's cold out here!

Knock knock.
Who's there?
Sheri.
Sheri who?
I'll Sheri my secret if you open the door!

Knock knock.
Who's there?
Abby.
Abby who?
Abby stung me on the leg—ouch!

Knock knock.
Who's there?
Abel.
Abel who?
Do you think you're Abel to
let me in now?

Knock knock.
Who's there?
Wallace.
Wallace who?
Wallace fair in love and war!

Knock knock.
Who's there?
Barry.
Barry who?
It's Barry nice to meet you!

Knock knock.
Who's there?
Isaac.
Isaac who?
Isaac of knocking, so please
let me in!

Knock knock.
Who's there?
Judith.
Judith who?
Judith thought these knock-
knock jokes would get
old, but they don't!

Knock knock.
Who's there?
Diane.
Diane who?
I'm Diane to see you, so
open the door!

Knock knock.
Who's there?
Carrie.
Carrie who?
Don't you Carrie that I'm
out here knocking?

Knock knock.
Who's there?
Taryn.
Taryn who?
It's Taryn me up inside that
you won't let me in!

Knock knock.
Who's there?
Annette.
Annette who?
**Annette to use the
bathroom, so please
open the door!**

Knock knock.
Who's there?
Whale.
Whale who?
**Whale, whale, whale, I see
your door is locked
again!**

Knock knock.
Who's there?
Art.
Art who?
**Art-2 D-2. May the force be
with you!**

Knock knock.
Who's there?
Dexter.
Dexter who?
**Dexter halls with boughs of
holly!**

Knock knock.
Who's there?
Hans.
Hans who?
**Hans up—you're under
arrest!**

Knock knock.
Who's there?
Delores.
Delores who?
**Delores my shepherd, I shall
not want.**

Knock knock.
Who's there?
Isabella.
Isabella who?
**Isabella the door not
working?**

Knock knock.
Who's there?
Don.
Don who?
**Don you want to come out
and play?**

Knock knock.
Who's there?
Woo.
Woo who?
Don't get all excited. It's just a knock-knock joke!

Knock knock.
Who's there?
Ketchup.
Ketchup who?
Let me come in so we can ketchup.

Knock knock.
Who's there?
Lego.
Lego who?
Lego of the doorknob so I can come in!

Knock knock.
Who's there?
Wa.
Wa who?
What are you so excited about?

Knock knock.
Who's there?
Howie.
Howie who?
Do you know Howie doing?

Knock knock.
Who's there?
Train.
Train who?
Someone needs to train you how to open a door.

Knock knock.
Who's there?
Cargo.
Cargo who?
Cargo beep, beep and vroom, vroom!

Knock knock.
Who's there?
Matt.
Matt who?
I'm standing on your welcome Matt, but I don't feel very welcome right now.

Knock knock.
> Who's there?

Nicole.
> Nicole who?

**I'll give you a Nicole if you
let me in.**

Knock knock.
> Who's there?

Sherwood.
> Sherwood who?

**Sherwood enjoy coming in
and seeing you!**

Knock knock.
> Who's there?

Ron.
> Ron who?

**You can Ron but you can't
hide!**

Knock knock.
> Who's there?

Andy.
> Andy who?

**He knocked Andy knocked,
but you won't let him in!**

Knock knock.
> Who's there?

Stan.
> Stan who?

Stan back, I'm coming in!

Knock knock.
> Who's there?

Henrietta.
> Henrietta who?

**Henrietta bug, and now he
has a stomachache.**

Knock knock.
> Who's there?

Hummus.
> Hummus who?

**Let me in and I'll hummus
a tune.**

Knock knock.
> Who's there?

I am.
> I am who?

**Don't you even know who
you are?**

Knock knock.
Who's there?
Hike.
Hike who?
**I didn't know you liked Japanese poetry.
(Haiku)**

Knock knock.
Who's there?
Pumpkin.
Pumpkin who?
A pumpkin fill up your flat tire.

Knock knock.
Who's there?
Darren.
Darren who?
I'm Darren you to tell a funnier knock-knock joke!

Knock knock.
Who's there?
Evie.
Evie who?
Evie wonder why I'm knocking at the door?

Knock knock.
Who's there?
Rufus.
Rufus who?
Call 911—the Rufus on fire!

Knock knock.
Who's there?
Wendy.
Wendy who?
Wendy last time you had your doorbell checked?

Knock knock.
Who's there?
Funnel.
Funnel who?
The funnel start once you let me in!

Knock knock.
Who's there?
I'm.
I'm who?
Don't you know your own name?

Knock knock.
    Who's there?
Hammond.
    Hammond who?
Let's make some Hammond
    eggs for breakfast.

Knock knock.
    Who's there?
Butcher.
    Butcher who?
Butcher hand over your
    heart when you say the
    pledge of allegiance.

Knock knock.
    Who's there?
Frank.
    Frank who?
Can I be Frank and say I
    really want you to open
    the door?

Knock knock.
    Who's there?
Peek-a.
    Peek-a who?
Peek-a-boo!

Knock knock.
    Who's there?
Passion.
    Passion who?
I was just passion through
    and thought I would say
    hello.

Knock knock.
    Who's there?
Pasture.
    Pasture who?
It's way pasture bedtime, so
    you'd better go to sleep!

Knock knock.
    Who's there?
Acid.
    Acid who?
Acid I would stop by, so
    here I am!

Knock knock.
    Who's there?
Elba.
    Elba who?
Elba happy to tell you
    another knock-knock
    joke!

Knock knock.
   Who's there?
Kent.
   Kent who?
I Kent see why you won't
   just open the door.

Knock knock.
   Who's there?
Zany.
   Zany who?
Zany body want to come out
   and play?

Knock knock.
   Who's there?
Brandy.
   Brandy who?
Cowboys Brandy cattle out
   on the ranch.

Knock knock.
   Who's there?
Dots.
   Dots who?
Dots for me to know and
   you to find out.

Knock knock.
   Who's there?
Frasier.
   Frasier who?
I'm a Frasier going to have
   to let me in eventually.

Knock knock.
   Who's there?
Woody.
   Woody who?
Woody like to hear another
   knock-knock joke?

Knock knock.
   Who's there?
Freeze.
   Freeze who?
Freeze a jolly good fellow,
   freeze a jolly good
   fellow.

Knock knock.
   Who's there?
Roy.
   Roy who?
Roy, Roy, Roy your boat
   gently down the stream.

Knock knock.
Who's there?
Wallaby.
Wallaby who?
Wallaby a monkey's uncle!

Knock knock.
Who's there?
Ivan.
Ivan who?
Ivan idea—let's tell more knock-knock jokes!

Knock knock.
Who's there?
Vera.
Vera who?
Is Vera way you could open the door?

Knock knock.
Who's there?
Snow.
Snow who?
Snow use—I'll never run out of knock-knock jokes!

Knock knock.
Who's there?
Bond.
Bond who?
You're bond to succeed if you try, try again.

Knock knock.
Who's there?
Bruce.
Bruce who?
I'll Bruce my knuckles if I keep on knocking!

Knock knock.
Who's there?
Elsie.
Elsie who?
Elsie you later!

Knock knock.
Who's there?
Luca.
Luca who?
Luca through the keyhole and you'll see who it is!

Knock knock.
Who's there?
Waddle.
Waddle who?
Waddle you give me if I stop
knocking and go away?

Knock knock.
Who's there?
Wade.
Wade who?
Wade a minute—I want to
tell you another knock-
knock joke!

Knock knock.
Who's there?
Megan.
Megan who?
It's Megan me mad that you
won't open the door!

Knock knock.
Who's there?
Ethan.
Ethan who?
Ethan if you don't open the
door, I'll still like you.

Knock knock.
Who's there?
Ima.
Ima who?
Ima waiting to hear another
knock-knock joke!

Knock knock.
Who's there?
Marilee.
Marilee who?
Marilee, Marilee, Marilee,
Marilee, life is but a
dream!

Knock knock.
Who's there?
Sorry.
Sorry who?
Sorry, I think I'm knocking
on the wrong door.

Knock knock.
Who's there?
Aaron.
Aaron who?
The Aaron here is kind of
stuffy.

Knock knock.
  Who's there?
Ben.
  Ben who?
**Ben away for a while, but
I'm back now.**

Knock knock.
  Who's there?
Cantaloupe.
  Cantaloupe who?
**You cantaloupe—you're too
young to get married!**

Knock knock.
  Who's there?
Stan.
  Stan who?
**I can't Stan it anymore,
tell me another knock-
knock joke.**

Knock knock.
  Who's there?
Taylor.
  Taylor who?
**Taylor another knock-knock
joke!**

Knock knock.
  Who's there?
Kay.
  Kay who?
**Is it O-Kay if I tell another
knock-knock joke?**

Knock knock.
  Who's there?
Ice cream soda.
  Ice cream soda who?
**Ice cream soda people can
hear me!**

Knock knock.
  Who's there?
Yugo.
  Yugo who?
**Yugo first, and I'll go
second.**

Knock knock.
  Who's there?
Vanessa.
  Vanessa who?
**Vanessa door going to open
up?**

Knock knock.
> Who's there?

Wilma.
> Wilma who?

**Wilma breakfast be ready
pretty soon?**

Knock knock.
> Who's there?

Macon.
> Macon who?

**I'm Macon my own key to
open this door!**

Knock knock.
> Who's there?

Rudy.
> Rudy who?

**It's Rudy never says please
or thank you.**

Knock knock.
> Who's there?

Bonnie.
> Bonnie who?

**My Bonnie lies over the
ocean.**

Knock knock.
> Who's there?

Theodore.
> Theodore who?

**Theodore is locked, so
please let me in!**

Knock knock.
> Who's there?

Anita.
> Anita who?

**Anita hear another knock-
knock joke!**

Knock knock.
> Who's there?

Olive.
> Olive who?

**Since Olive here, I think you
should let me in!**

Knock knock.
> Who's there?

Sadie.
> Sadie who?

**If I Sadie magic word
will you let me in . . .
P-L-E-A-S-E?**

Knock knock.
Who's there?
Michael.
Michael who?
I Michael you on the phone if you don't answer the door!

Knock knock.
Who's there?
Bill.
Bill who?
I'll pay the Bill for dinner if you open the door!

Knock knock.
Who's there?
Francis.
Francis who?
Francis in Europe, and Brazil is in South America.

Knock knock.
Who's there?
Tokyo.
Tokyo who?
What Tokyo so long to open the door?

Knock knock.
Who's there?
Olive.
Olive who?
Olive you!

Knock knock.
Who's there?
Colin.
Colin who?
From now on I'm Colin you on the phone!

Knock knock.
Who's there?
Sarah.
Sarah who?
Sarah reason you're not opening the door?

Knock knock.
Who's there?
Donut.
Donut who?
Donut make you laugh when people tell knock-knock jokes?

Knock knock.
Who's there?
Mummy.
Mummy who?
Mummy said you can come out and play.

Knock knock.
Who's there?
Muffin.
Muffin who?
Muffin much going on around here.

Knock knock.
Who's there?
Coke.
Coke who?
Are you calling me crazy?

Knock knock.
Who's there?
Waffle.
Waffle who?
It's waffle that you still haven't opened the door!

Knock knock.
Who's there?
Fannie.
Fannie who?
If Fannie body calls, tell them I went to the store.

Knock knock.
Who's there?
Kanga.
Kanga who?
No, kangaroo.

Knock knock.
Who's there?
Noah.
Noah who?
Noah don't think I'll tell you another knock-knock joke!

Knock knock.
Who's there?
Leaf.
Leaf who?
Leaf me alone so I can read my joke book!

Knock knock.
  Who's there?
Della.
  Della who?
**Open the door so I can
  Della another knock-
  knock joke.**

Knock knock.
  Who's there?
Reed.
  Reed who?
Reed a good book lately?

Knock knock.
  Who's there?
Walt.
  Walt who?
Walt! Who goes there?

Knock knock.
  Who's there?
Philip.
  Philip who?
**Philip your water bottle if
  you're thirsty.**

Knock knock.
  Who's there?
Hawaii.
  Hawaii who?
**I'm doing fine, thanks.
  Hawaii doing?**

Knock knock.
  Who's there?
Fanny.
  Fanny who?
Fanny you should ask!

Knock knock.
  Who's there?
Lorraine.
  Lorraine who?
**Lorraine is coming down, so
  give me an umbrella!**

Knock knock.
  Who's there?
Randy.
  Randy who?
**I Randy whole way here, so
  open up!**

Knock knock.
   Who's there?
Reggie.
   Reggie who?
**Reggie to open the door
   yet?**

Knock knock.
   Who's there? .
Rich.
   Rich who?
**Rich knock-knock joke is
   your favorite?**

Knock knock.
   Who's there?
Dwight.
   Dwight who?
**Dwight key will get the door
   open.**

Knock knock.
   Who's there?
Chad.
   Chad who?
**Chad don't you recognize
   me? I'm your son!**

Knock knock.
   Who's there?
Landon.
   Landon who?
**Is it true cats always Landon
   their feet?**

Knock knock.
   Who's there?
Les.
   Les who?
**Les you think I'm a stranger,
   look through the
   keyhole and you will
   see.**

Knock knock.
   Who's there?
Meg.
   Meg who?
**Meg up your mind—are
   you going to let me in or
   aren't you?**

Knock knock.
Who's there
Doris.
Doris who?
**If the Doris locked, I can't
come in.**

Knock knock.
Who's there?
New Hampshire.
New Hampshire who?
**New Hampshire you're not
going to open the door.**

Knock knock.
Who's there?
Macon.
Macon who?
**You're Macon me mad with
all this knocking I'm
having to do!**

Knock knock.
Who's there?
Yukon.
Yukon who?
It's okay, Yukon tell me!

Knock knock.
Who's there?
Watson.
Watson who?
Watson TV tonight?

Knock knock.
Who's there?
Pig.
Pig who?
**I'm going to pig the lock if
you don't open the door
and let me in!**

Knock knock.
Who's there?
Juno.
Juno who?
**Juno who this is, so open up
already!**

Knock knock.
Who's there?
Albert.
Albert who?
**Do Alberts fly south for the
winter?**

Knock knock.
Who's there?
Alvin.
Alvin who?
We're Alvin a great time out
here!

Knock knock.
Who's there?
Figs.
Figs who?
Figs your phone so I can
give you a call!

Knock knock.
Who's there?
Alma.
Alma who?
Alma knock-knock jokes are
really funny!

Knock knock.
Who's there?
Alex.
Alex who?
Alex the questions around
here!

Knock knock.
Who's there?
Sherwood.
Sherwood who?
Sherwood be nice if you'd
open the door.

Knock knock.
Who's there?
Abbott.
Abbott who?
Abbott time you asked!

Knock knock.
Who's there?
Abel.
Abel who?
Abel rings every time an
angel gets its wings.

Knock knock.
Who's there?
Annette.
Annette who?
Annette another glass of
water, open up!

Knock knock.
 Who's there?
To.
 To who?
To whom!

Knock knock.
 Who's there?
Pizza.
 Pizza who?
Pizza really nice guy.

Knock knock.
 Who's there?
Mickey.
 Mickey who?
Mickey won't unlock this
 door, so please let me
 in!

Knock knock.
 Who's there?
Cash.
 Cash who?
No thanks, I'd rather have
 some peanuts.

Knock knock.
 Who's there?
Luke.
 Luke who?
Luke through the window
 and you'll see who's
 knocking.

Knock knock.
 Who's there?
Roach.
 Roach who?
I roach you a letter, but I
 wanted to deliver it in
 person.

Knock knock.
 Who's there?
Abby.
 Abby who?
Abby birthday to you, Abby
 birthday to you!

Knock knock.
Who's there?
Alberta.
Alberta who?
Alberta can't guess in a
million years!

Knock knock.
Who's there?
Anna.
Anna who?
Anna one, Anna two, Anna
three!

Knock knock.
Who's there?
Dozen.
Dozen who?
Dozen anyone ever open
their door anymore?

Knock knock.
Who's there?
Hair.
Hair who?
Hair today and gone
tomorrow.

Knock knock.
Who's there?
Ken.
Ken who?
Ken you hear me now?

Knock knock.
Who's there?
Alpaca.
Alpaca who?
Alpaca suitcase for our
vacation.

Knock knock.
Who's there?
Dishes.
Dishes who?
Dishes me, open up!

Knock knock.
Who's there?
Candice.
Candice who?
Candice joke get any worse?

Knock knock.
  Who's there?
Tibet.
  Tibet who?
Early Tibet, early to rise.

Knock knock.
  Who's there?
Tank.
  Tank who?
You're welcome!

Knock knock.
  Who's there?
Andy.
  Andy who?
Andy shoots, Andy scores!

Knock knock.
  Who's there?
Owls.
  Owls who?
Why yes, they do!

Knock knock.
  Who's there?
Otter.
  Otter who?
**You otter open the door and
  let me in!**

Knock knock.
  Who's there?
Bacon.
  Bacon who?
**I'm bacon some cookies. Do
  you want one?**

Knock knock.
  Who's there?
Haven.
  Haven who?
**Haven you heard enough
  of these knock-knock
  jokes?**

Knock knock.
  Who's there?
Anita.
  Anita who?
**Anita drink of water, so
  please let me in!**

Josh:	**Knock knock.**
Leah:	Who's there?
Josh:	**Banana.**
Leah:	Banana who?
Josh:	**Knock knock.**
Leah:	Who's there?
Josh:	**Banana.**
Leah:	Banana who?
Josh:	**Knock knock.**
Leah:	Who's there?
Josh:	**Banana.**
Leah:	Banana who?
Josh:	**Knock knock.**
Leah:	Who's there?
Josh:	**Orange.**
Leah:	Orange who?
Josh:	**Orange you glad this joke is over?**

Knock knock.
Who's there?
Pitcher.
Pitcher who?
Bless you! Are you catching a cold?

Knock knock.
Who's there?
Alex.
Alex who?
Alex-plain when you open the door!

Knock knock.
Who's there?
Elsie.
Elsie who?
Elsie you later!

Knock knock.
Who's there?
Ears.
Ears who?
Ears looking at you, kid.

Knock knock.
Who's there?
Lydia.
Lydia who?
The Lydia fell off and made a big mess out here; please open up.

Knock knock.
Who's there?
Nun.
Nun who?
Nun of your business.

Knock knock.
Who's there?
June.
June who?
June know how long I've been knocking out here?

Knock knock.
Who's there?
August.
August who?
August of wind almost blew me away!

Knock knock.
Who's there?
Spell.
Spell who?
W-H-O.

Knock knock.
Who's there?
Police.
Police who?
Police come out and play
with me!

Knock knock.
Who's there?
Jamaica.
Jamaica who?
Jamaica good sandwich? I'm
hungry!

Knock knock.
Who's there?
Ally.
Ally who?
Ally really want to do is tell
another knock-knock
joke!

Knock knock.
Who's there?
Eve.
Eve who?
I'll Eve you alone if you
want me to.

Knock knock.
Who's there?
Whale.
Whale who?
I'll start to whale if you
don't let me in.

Knock knock.
Who's there?
Ima.
Ima who?
Ima really glad to see you
today!

Knock knock.
Who's there?
Jonah.
Jonah who?
Jonah anybody who will
open the door for me?

Knock knock.
Who's there?
Cain.
Cain who?
Cain you open the door for me, it's very cold out here!

Knock knock.
Who's there?
Dishes.
Dishes who?
Dishes a really dumb knock-knock joke!

Knock knock.
Who's there?
Ada.
Ada who?
Ada lot of sweets, and now I feel sick!

Knock knock.
Who's there?
Adam.
Adam who?
Adam all up and see how much you have!

Knock knock.
Who's there?
Jell-o.
Jell-o who?
Jell-o, it's me again!

Knock knock.
Who's there?
Barbie.
Barbie who?
Barbie-Q.

Knock knock.
Who's there?
Peas.
Peas who?
Peas come outside and play with me!

Knock knock.
Who's there?
Fanny.
Fanny who?
If Fanny body asks, tell them I'm not home.

Knock knock.
    Who's there?
Jess.
    Jess who?
Jess me and my shadow.

Knock knock.
    Who's there?
Baby oil.
    Baby oil who?
Baby oil will, and baby oil
    won't!

Knock knock.
    Who's there?
Canoe.
    Canoe who?
Canoe come out and play?

Knock knock.
    Who's there?
Oldest.
    Oldest who?
Oldest knocking is giving
    me a headache.

Knock knock.
    Who's there?
Woody.
    Woody who?
Woody like to hear another
    knock-knock joke?

Knock knock.
    Who's there?
Weed.
    Weed who?
Weed better go home—it's
    time for dinner!

Knock knock.
    Who's there?
Juan.
    Juan who?
I Juan to tell you another
    knock-knock joke.

Knock knock.
    Who's there?
Anita.
    Anita who?
Anita minute to think of
    another knock-knock
    joke.

Knock knock.
Who's there?
Amos.
Amos who?
Amos-quito bit me on the arm!

Knock knock.
Who's there?
Andy.
Andy who?
Andy bit me again.

Knock knock.
Who's there?
Colin.
Colin who?
I'll be Colin you later.

Knock knock.
Who's there?
Rockefeller.
Rockefeller who?
You can Rockefeller to sleep in his cradle.

Knock knock
Who's there?
Water.
Water who?
Water your favorite knock-knock jokes?

Knock knock.
Who's there?
Conner.
Conner who?
Conner tell me another joke that's as funny as the last one?

Knock knock.
Who's there?
Dragon.
Dragon who?
Quit dragon your feet and open the door!

Knock knock.
Who's there?
Ringo.
Ringo who?
Ringo round the rosie!

Knock knock.
Who's there?
Willie.
Willie who?
**Willie ever open the door
and let me in?**

Knock knock.
Who's there?
Wanda.
Wanda who?
**I Wanda where I put my car
keys.**

Knock knock.
Who's there?
Moe.
Moe who?
**Moe knock-knock jokes,
please!**

Knock knock.
Who's there?
Ernest.
Ernest who?
Ernest is full of eggs!

Knock knock.
Who's there?
Taylor.
Taylor who?
**Taylor brother to pick up
his toys.**

Knock knock.
Who's there?
Dewy.
Dewy who?
**Dewy have a key to open
this door, or do I have
to go through the
window?**

Knock knock.
Who's there?
Lettuce.
Lettuce who?
**Lettuce know when you can
come out and play!**

Knock knock.
    Who's there?
Nose.
    Nose who?
Nose anymore good knock-
    knock jokes?

Knock knock.
    Who's there?
Watt.
    Watt who?
Watt, you want to hear
    another knock-knock
    joke?

Knock knock.
    Who's there?
Juicy.
    Juicy who?
Juicy any monsters under
    my bed?

Knock knock.
    Who's there?
Yellow.
    Yellow who?
Yellow, how are you doing
    today?

Knock knock.
    Who's there?
Raymond.
    Raymond who?
Raymond me to buy milk at
    the store.

Knock knock.
    Who's there?
Doughnut.
    Doughnut who?
Doughnut open the door to
    strangers!

Knock knock.
    Who's there?
Handsome.
    Handsome who?
Handsome snacks over
    here—I'm really
    hungry!

Knock knock.
    Who's there?
Rabbit.
    Rabbit who?
Rabbit carefully—it's a
    special present!

Knock knock.
Who's there?
Sarah.
Sarah who?
Is Sarah a doctor in the house?

Knock knock.
Who's there?
Oscar.
Oscar who?
Oscar silly question and get a silly answer!

Knock knock.
Who's there?
Who.
Who who?
What, are you an owl or something?

Knock knock.
Who's there?
Gorilla.
Gorilla who?
Gorilla me a hamburger, I'm hungry!

Knock knock.
Who's there?
Conrad.
Conrad who?
Conrad-ulations! That was a great knock-knock joke!

Knock knock.
Who's there?
Walter.
Walter who?
Walter you doing here so early?

Knock knock.
Who's there?
Everest.
Everest who?
Everest, or is it work, work, work?

Knock knock.
Who's there?
Lion.
Lion who?
Quit lion around and open the door!

Knock knock.
  Who's there?
Thatcher.
  Thatcher who?
**Thatcher was a good knock-
  knock joke. Can you tell
  another one?**

Knock knock.
  Who's there?
Peace.
  Peace who?
**Peace porridge hot, peace
  porridge cold.**

4

MORE LAUGH -OUT- LOUD JOKES for KIDS

Knock knock.

Who's there?

Chew.

Chew who?

I want to hang out with chew so let me in!

Mark:	**What's the best place to chop down a Christmas tree?**
Tim:	I'm not sure.
Mark:	**About three inches off the ground.**

Q: Why did the broccoli slap the lettuce?

A: Because it was being fresh!

Q: Why did the elephants take up the least amount of room on Noah's ark?

A: Because they kept everything in their trunks!

Q: Why did the moon feel sick to its stomach?

A: It was a full moon.

Suzy: **I'm so smart I can sing the whole alphabet song!**

Jimmy: That's nothing. I can sing it in lower case and capitals!

Q: Why were the lamb and goat such good friends?

A: Because they had a very close relation-sheep.

Q: What do you get when you spill your coffee in the dirt?

A: Coffee grounds!

Q: What kind of vegetable has the worst manners?

A: A rude-abaga.

Q: What is penguin's favorite kind of food?

A: Ice-burgers.

Q: What do you get when you brush your teeth with dish soap?

A: Bubble gums.

Q: What kind of trees wear mittens?

A: Palm trees.

Q: Why was the library so busy?

A: It was overbooked.

Q: **What do you get when you cross a porcupine with a snail?**

A: A slowpoke.

Q: **When do farmers go bald?**

A: When they have re-seeding hairlines.

Q: **How do you know when it's been raining cats and dogs?**

A: When you step in a poodle.

> **Justin:** **Do you know how to make a pineapple shake?**
>
> **Nate:** You mix pineapple, milk, and ice cream?
>
> **Justin:** **No, you take it to a scary movie!**

Q: **What do you get when you cross an owl and bubble gum?**

A: A bird that will chews wisely.

Knock knock.

Who's there?

Leon.

Leon who?

I'd be Leon if I told you I didn't love knock-knock jokes!

Q: What kind of homework do you do on the couch?

A: Multipli-cushion.

> **Tim:** Did you hear about the guy who stuck his finger in a light socket?
>
> **Scott:** No, what happened?
>
> **Tim:** It was shocking!

Q: How does a cow get to the office?

A: On a cow-moo-ter train.

Q: What do you get when you cross a dinosaur and gunpowder?

A: Dino-mite.

Q: Why shouldn't you stare at the turkey dressing at Thanksgiving?

A: The turkey will be embarrassed.

Q: Why did the skeleton refuse to go to the dance?

A: He had no-body to dance with.

Q: Why did the suspenders have to go to jail?

A: They held up a pair of pants.

Q: Why don't fish ever get a summer vacation?

A: They spend every day in schools.

Q: What do you get when you play tug-of-war with a pig?

A: Pulled pork.

Joe: Can you believe that I ate six helpings of spaghetti last night?

Bill: Well, I wouldn't put it pasta!

Q: Why did the orange have to stop and take a nap?

A: It ran out of juice.

Q: What do you call a boomerang that won't come back to you?

A: A stick.

Q: Did you hear about the new restaurant they put on Mars?

A: I hear the food is out of this world.

Q: How much did Santa pay for his reindeer?

A: Just a few bucks. They didn't cost him much doe.

Q: What is a trumpet player's favorite month of the year?

A: March.

Sally: What is a mummy's favorite kind of music?

Bill: I'm not sure.

Sally: Wrap music!

Q: Why couldn't the fish go shopping?

A: It didn't have anemone.

Andrew: Do you know how to spell "hard water" using only three letters?

Dave: I'm pretty sure that's impossible!

Andrew: No, it isn't. I-C-E is hard water!

Q: What kind of motorcycle do bulls like to ride?

A: They ride a Cow-asaki.

Q: What does a grizzly do on a hard day?

A: He'll just grin and bear it.

Q: How many months have 28 days?

A: All twelve of them do!

Knock knock.

Who's there?

Bean.

Bean who?

Its bean way too long since you've heard a knock-knock joke!

Q: What do you call a pumpkin that watches over you?

A: A body-gourd.

Q: What do you call a greasy bug?

A: A butter-fly.

Q: Why did the whale cross the ocean?

A: To get to the other tide.

Q: Why did the rabbit need to relax?

A: He was feeling jumpy.

Q: Why did the skunk cross the road?

A: To get to the odor side!

Q: What do you get when you combine an elephant and a skunk?

A: A smell-ephant.

Q: What kind of vegetable is hip and cool?

A: A radish.

Q: How do you sneak across the desert without being seen?

A: You wear camel-flage.

Q: What is a maple's favorite class at school?

A: Geometree.

Knock knock.

Who's there?

Arthur.

Arthur who?

Arthur any more funny knock-knock jokes?

Q: Why wouldn't the turkey eat any pumpkin pie?

A: It was too stuffed.

Q: What do you call bears with no ears?

A: B!

Q: What happened when the turkey got in a fight?

A: He got the stuffing knocked out of him.

Knock knock.

Who's there?

Annie.

Annie who?

Annie chance I could tell you another knock-knock joke?

Q: What does a black belt eat for lunch?
A: Kung food!

Q: Why did the lobster get grounded by his parents?
A: He was always getting himself in hot water!

Q: What kind of automobile is the same going backward and forward?
A: Racecar.

Knock knock.

Who's there?

Gus.

Gus who?

I bet you can't Gus who this is!

Q: **What did the skunks do on Saturday night?**

A: They watched a movie on their smell-evision.

Q: **What do you call bunny's prized possessions?**

A: Hare-looms.

Q: **What do you get when you combine a kitty and a fish?**

A: A purr-anha!

Q: **What do fish like to sing during the holidays?**

A: Christmas corals.

Q: **What do you get when you drop a pumpkin from your roof?**

A: Squash.

Q: **Why did the apples want to hang out with the banana?**

A: Because it was so appeeling.

Q: **Why couldn't the skeletons play any music?**

A: They didn't have any organs.

Adel: My math book fell into my jack-o'-lantern the other day.

Anna: What did you do?

Adel: I made pumpkin pi.

Q: What did the blackbird use to get the door open?

A: A crow bar!

Q: What do you call kids who play outside in the snow?

A: Chilled-ren.

Q: What did the almond say to the psychiatrist?

A: "Everybody says I'm nuts!"

Q: Why was the skeleton laughing?

A: Somebody tickled its funny bone.

Q: How do you keep a restaurant safe from criminals?

A: Use a burger alarm.

Q: What does a cat eat for breakfast?

A: Mice Krispies.

Q: How does a pig get to the hospital?

A: In a ham-bulance.

Q: What do you get when you cross a dog and broccoli?

A: Collie-flower.

Q: What language do pigs speak?

A: French, because they go "Oui, oui, oui," all the way home!

Q: What has a head and a tail, but no body?

A: A penny.

Q: What do you feed a teddy bear?

A: Stuffing!

Q: Why did the elf get in trouble with his teacher?

A: He didn't do his gnomework.

Q: What do you get when you cross a snake with dessert?

A: A pie-thon.

Dave: What do you get when you cross an airplane, a car, and a cat?

Bill: I give up.

Dave: A flying car-pet!

Q: What kind of homework do you do in a taxi?

A: Vocabulary.

Q: **What has a face and two hands, but no arms or legs?**

A: A clock!

Q: **How do you make friends with everyone at school?**

A: Become the princi-pal.

Q: **What do you get when you play basketball in Hawaii?**

A: Hula-Hoops!

Q: **What is a snowman's favorite cereal?**

A: Frosted Flakes.

Q: **What do you call a boy with no money in his pocket?**

A: Nickel-less.

Q: **How did the oyster get to the doctor?**

A: In a clam-bulance.

Q: **Why was the snake so funny?**

A: His jokes were hiss-terical.

Knock knock.

Who's there?

Whale.

Whale who?

Whale you let me tell you another knock-knock joke?

Q: What is a sailor's favorite kind of book to read?
A: Ferry tales.

Q: Which word in the dictionary is always spelled wrong?
A: WRONG, of course!

Q: What does a monster put on top of his hot fudge sundae?
A: Whipped scream.

Q: Why did the burglar steal the eggs?
A: He likes his eggs poached!

Q: Why can't you ever trust an atom?
A: They make up everything!

Q: Why did the chef have to stop cooking?
A: He ran out of thyme.

Q: What is an elephant's favorite vegetable?

A: Squash.

Q: How do frogs get the ice off their car windows?

A: They use the defrogger.

Q: How do you know if you have an elephant in your refrigerator?

A: The refrigerator door won't shut!

Q: What did the tornado say to the race car?

A: "Can I take you for a spin?"

Q: What does a weasel like to read?

A: Pop-up books!

Q: What is a squirrel's favorite ballet?

A: The Nutcracker!

Q: How did everyone know that the lion swallowed the bear?

A: His stomach was growling.

Q: What do frogs like with their cheeseburgers?

A: French flies and a croak.

Q: What is the best thing to do with a blue whale?

A: Tell it a joke and cheer it up!

Q: What happened to the dog after it swallowed the watch?

A: It was full of ticks.

Q: What kind of shoes do foxes wear?

A: Sneak-ers.

Q: What did the baker say when his cookie wouldn't crumble?

A: "That's one tough cookie!"

Q: What did the bee say to the flower?

A: "Hi, honey!"

Q: What did the flower say to the bee?

A: "Buzz off!"

Q: What did the picture say when the police showed up?

A: "I didn't do it—I've been framed!"

Q: Why did the king go to the dentist?

A: Because he wanted a crown on his tooth!

Q: Why was the comedian sad?

A: He thought his life was a joke!

Knock knock.

Who's there?

Auto.

Auto who?

You really auto tell me some knock-knock jokes!

Q: Why did the book join the police force?

A: It wanted to go undercover!

Q: What do you get when you cross a bird and a bee?

A: A buzzard.

Q: Why did the elephant quit his job?

A: He was working for peanuts.

Q: What do you get when you throw a couch in the pond?

A: A sitting duck!

Q: What do you get when you cross a horse and a pencil?

A: Horseback writing.

Q: Why did the policeman go to the baseball game?

A: He heard someone had stolen second base.

Q: What kinds of keys are easy to swallow?

A: Cookies.

Knock knock.

Who's there?

Ken.

Ken who?

Ken I tell you another knock-knock joke?

Q: Why did the horse go to the psychiatrist?

A: It was feeling un-stable.

Q: What kind of sea creatures are the most musical?

A: Fish, because they have so many scales!

Q: When do you know a tiger isn't telling the truth?

A: When it's a lion.

Q: Why did the baker go to work every day?

A: He really kneaded the dough!

Q: **What did the bumblebee say to his wife?**

A: "Honey, you're bee-utiful."

Q: **Where does a cow go when it's hungry?**

A: To the calf-eteria.

Knock knock.

Who's there?

Tibet.

Tibet who?

Early Tibet, early to rise.

Bob: **Did you hear about the farmer who wrote a joke book?**

Bill: No, is it any good?

Bob: **The jokes are really corn-y.**

Q: **What does a moose like to play at parties?**

A: Moose-ical chairs.

Q: **Who leads the orchestra at the zoo?**

A: The boa-conductor.

Q: **What did the drum say to the violin?**
A: "Stop harping at me!"

Q: **What do little cows give?**
A: Condensed milk.

Q: **What does a possum like to do for fun?**
A: Hang out with its friends!

Q: **Who helped the mermaid go to the ball?**
A: Her fairy cod-mother.

Knock knock.

    Who's there?

Hector.

    Hector who?

When the Hector you going to open the door?

Q: **What does a snowman eat for dessert?**
A: Ice krispy treats.

Emma: **Can February March?**
Leah: No, but April May.

Q: What do you call someone with no body and no nose?

A: No-body knows.

Q: Which has more courage, a rock or a tree?

A: A rock—it's boulder!

Q: Why did the plant go to the dentist?

A: It needed a root canal!

Josh: **Do you think change is hard?**

Joe: I sure do—have you ever tried to bend a quarter?

Patient: **Hey doc, I think I broke my leg in two places. What should I do?**

Doctor: Don't go to those two places anymore!

Knock knock.

Who's there?

Minnow.

Minnow who?

If you can think of a better knock-knock joke, let minnow.

John: I'm really bright.

Jane: How bright are you?

John: I'm so bright, my mother calls me sun.

Jill: I'm upset that my new toaster isn't waterproof.

Jen: What's so bad about that?

Jill: When I found out, I was shocked!

Q: How do fleas travel from one dog to another?

A: They itchhike their way there!

Q: What is a swan's favorite Christmas carol?

A: Duck the Halls.

Q: Why did the chicken go to bed?

A: It was eggs-hausted.

Knock knock.

Who's there?

Gas.

Gas who?

I bet you can't gas who this is at the door!

Q: What is something that has to be broken before you can use it?

A: An egg!

Knock knock.

Who's there?

Window.

Window who?

Window you want to hear another great knock-knock joke?

Bill: Do you know who told me you sound like an owl when you talk?

Joe: No, who?

Q: What did the fork say to the butter knife?

A: "You're so dull."

Q: What do you get from an invisible cow?

A: Evaporated milk.

Q: What do you get when you cross a dentist and a boat?

A: A tooth ferry.

Q: **Why did the boy eat his homework?**
A: The teacher said it would be a piece of cake.

Q: **Why did the banana put on sunscreen?**
A: It didn't want to peel.

Q: **Why did the Starburst go to school?**
A: It wanted to be a Smartie.

Patient: **Doc, I think I'm turning into a piano.**
Doc: Well, that's just grand!

Q: **Where do you learn to cut wood?**
A: At boarding school.

Q: **Where does a volcano wash its hands?**
A: In the lava-tory.

Q: **Why did the wheel stop turning?**
A: It was too tired.

Q: **What goes up but doesn't come back down?**
A: Your age!

Q: How did the pig write a letter?

A: With a pig pen.

Q: Which giraffe won the race?

A: It was a tie—they were neck and neck the whole time.

Q: What does a pig use when it has a rash?

A: Oinkment.

Q: Why did the tree need to take a nap?

A: It was bushed.

Knock knock.

Who's there?

Pecan.

Pecan who?

You should pecan someone your own size!

Q: What has four wheels and flies?

A: A garbage truck!

Q: What is the worst day of the week for fish?

A: Fryday!

Q: **What kind of buttons does everyone wear?**
A: Belly buttons.

Q: **How do you repair a squashed tomato?**
A: Use tomato paste!

Q: **What is a soda's favorite subject in school?**
A: Fizzics.

Q: **What sometimes runs but never walks?**
A: Your nose!

Q: **What is a cow's favorite painting?**
A: The Moona Lisa.

Knock knock.

Who's there?

Rita.

Rita who?

Did you Rita good book lately?

Knock knock.

Who's there?

Ears.

Ears who?

Ears looking at you, kid.

Q: What is the best time to see the dentist?
A: At tooth-thirty.

Q: What kind of tree needs a doctor all the time?
A: A sycamore tree.

Q: Why did the bathtub need a vacation?
A: Because it was drained.

Q: What kind of vegetable is lazy and irresponsible?
A: A dead-beet.

Q: Why did the meteorite go to Hollywood?
A: It wanted to be a star.

Q: What do you get when you cross a snowman and a lion?
A: Frost-bite.

Q: What do you get when you throw noodles in a Jacuzzi?

A: Spa-ghetti.

Q: When is a cow happy, then sad, and then angry?

A: When it's moo-dy.

Q: What did the ocean say to the fishing boat?

A: Nothing—it just waved.

Q: Which of Santa's reindeer has the worst manners?

A: Rude-olph.

Q: Why did the inventor get struck by lightning?

A: He was brain-storming.

Q: What did the one maple leaf say to the other maple leaf?

A: "I'm falling for you!"

Q: Why did the stereo explode?

A: It was radio-active.

Q: How do you know when a bucket is feeling sick?

A: When it looks a little pail.

Q: What plays music on your head?

A: A head-band.

Q: What kind of bird do you have with every meal?

A: A swallow.

Q: What do you call a lion that gives you presents?

A: Santa Claws.

Q: What do you get when you cross a flower, a car, and the USA?

A: A pink car nation.

Q: What did Mrs. Claus say to Santa when he was complaining about the rain on Christmas Eve?

A: "Oh, let it rain, dear."

Q: What's a hyena's favorite kind of cookie?

A: A snickerdoodle.

Q: Why can't a beaver use a computer?

A: It doesn't know how to log in.

Q: What do you call your dog when it goes deaf?

A: It doesn't matter—it can't hear you anyway!

Q: How much did Santa's sleigh cost?

A: Nothing—it was on the house!

Q: What is a skeleton's favorite instrument?

A: A trombone.

Q: Why didn't the panda bear get the job?

A: It didn't have the right koala-fications.

> **Sally:** Can you believe I gave my pigs a bath?
>
> **Susie:** That's a bunch of hog wash!

Q: Why did the clock go back four seconds?

A: It was really hungry!

Q: Why did the lobster need crutches?

A: It pulled a mussel.

Q: Why did the book have to go to the hospital?

A: To have its appendix removed.

> **Jim:** I want to build a gigantic boat, but I'll need some help.
>
> **Bob:** Well, I just happen to Noah guy.

Q: When is a noodle a fake?

A: When it's an im-pasta.

Q: What has four legs but can't walk?

A: A chair.

Q: Why do silent frogs live forever?

A: Because they never croak!

Tammy: I'm embarrassed to go to the eye doctor.

Tommy: Why?

Tammy: My doctor always makes a spectacle of himself!

Q: How does a bumblebee stay out of trouble?

A: It stays on its best bee-havior.

Q: When does a hot dog get on your nerves?

A: When it's being a brat—it's the wurst.

Jimmy: Did you hear about the kid that got hit in the head with a can of pop?

Bobby: No, is he ok?

Jimmy: Yep, he's just lucky it was a soft drink.

Emma: I'm reading a book about gravity.

Leah: That's cool. Is it a good book?

Emma: It sure is! I just can't put it down.

Q: Why did the boy stop using his pencil?

A: It was pointless.

Q: Why did the ruler have a bad report card?

A: His grades just didn't measure up.

Q: Why did the wood fall asleep?

A: It was board.

Q: What do you get when you cross a train with a tissue?

A: An achoo-choo train.

Q: Why did the bee need to take allergy medicine?

A: It had lots of hives.

Q: What happens when strawberries are sad?

A: They become blueberries!

Q: What did the judge say to the skunk?

A: "Odor in the court!"

Q: Why was the potato chip mad at the pretzel?

A: Because it was insalting him.

Q: Why can you trust your secrets with a sea lion?

A: Their lips are always seal-ed!

Q: What did the lipstick say to the eye shadow?

A: "We should stop fighting and make-up!"

Q: Where do astronauts keep their sandwiches?

A: In their launch-box.

Q: Why was the man upset after he became a vegetarian?

A: He realized he'd made a missed-steak.

Sam: Did you like that story about the farm?

Sue: No, it didn't have a very good plot.

Q: Why couldn't the Cyclops family get along?

A: They could never see eye-to-eye.

Knock knock.

Who's there?

Bat.

Bat who?

I bat you want to hear some more knock-knock jokes!

Q: What did the shovel say to the sand?
A: "I really dig you!"

Q: Who helps pigs fall in love?
A: Cu-pig.

Q: How do bees get to school?
A: They take the school buzz.

Q: Why can't you tell a joke to an egg?
A: It might crack up!

Q: Why didn't the two 4's come to the dinner table?
A: Because they already 8.

Q: Why was the carpenter mad that he hit the nail with his hammer?
A: Because it was his fingernail!

Knock knock.

Who's there?

Bach.

Bach who?

I'll be Bach later when you're ready to open the door!

Knock knock.

Who's there?

Lasagna.

Lasagna who?

Are you going to lasagna couch all day, or are you going to answer the door?

Knock knock.

Who's there?

Snow.

Snow who?

What, don't you snow me?

Knock knock.

Who's there?

Bacon.

Bacon who?

Don't go bacon my heart.

Q: What kind of bugs like to sneak up on you?
A: Spy-ders.

Q: What do magicians like to eat for breakfast?
A: Trix cereal.

Knock knock.

Who's there?

Shore.

Shore who?

I shore hope you know some more knock-knock jokes!

Knock knock.

Who's there?

Minnow.

Minnow who?

Let minnow when you plan on letting me in!

Q: What kind of cars do deep-sea divers drive?
A: Scubarus.

Q: What is a whale's motto?
A: "Seas the Day."

Q: Why did the shoe fall in love with the boot?
A: Because they were sole mates.

Knock knock.

Who's there?

Roach.

Roach who?

I roach you a letter—will you write back soon?

Q: Why was the snail moving so slow?
A: It was feeling sluggish.

Q: Why did the frog get sent home from school?

A: He was a bully-frog!

Q: What happened when they invented the broom?

A: It was an idea that swept the nation!

Q: How does Moses make his tea?

A: Hebrews it.

Q: Why do cows wear cowbells?

A: Because they don't have horns.

Q: What kind of dogs are always on time?

A: Watch dogs!

Q: What is the best way to communicate with a fish?

A: Drop it a line.

Q: How does Jack Frost get around?

A: On his motor-cicle.

Q: What do you get when you cross a bear and a pig?

A: A grizzly boar!

Q: **When should you stay away from a comedian?**

A: When they want to give you the punch-line!

Q: **How did the marching band keep their teeth clean?**

A: With a tuba toothpaste.

Q: **Why wouldn't the lions play games with the zebras?**

A: There were too many cheetahs.

Q: **How do comedians like their eggs?**

A: Funny-side up.

Knock knock.

Who's there?

Moe.

Moe who?

Do you know any Moe knock-knock jokes?

Q: **Why is the ocean so much fun?**

A: You can always have a whale of a time.

Q: **When can't you believe anything a hippopotamus says?**

A: When it's a hippo-crite.

Knock knock.

Who's there?

Taco.

Taco who?

I don't want to taco 'bout it—just let me in!

Q: What did the violin say to the guitar when it was worried?
A: "Don't fret!"

Q: Why are omelets so out of shape?
A: They don't get enough eggs-ercise.

Q: Why didn't the cow have any money?
A: The farmer had milked it for all its worth!

Peter: You have got to put pickles on your sandwich!
Penny: Why, what's the big dill?

Q: What did the C note say to the D note?
A: "Stop! You're under a rest."

Q: How do you know if your printer likes music?
A: When it's always jamming.

Knock knock.

Who's there?

Bacon.

Bacon who?

Let me in—I'm bacon out here!

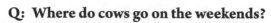

Q: Where do cows go on the weekends?
A: To the moo-seum.

Q: When does a king have trouble breathing?
A: When he doesn't have any heir.

Q: What do you give a deer with a tummy ache?
A: Elk-aseltzer.

Q: Why did the bear eat a lamp?
A: It just wanted a light snack.

Q: Where did the beaver put its money?
A: In the river bank.

Q: Why did the house go to the doctor?
A: It had a lot of window panes.

Q: Why was the bee's hair all sticky?

A: It used a honeycomb.

Q: What do you get when you try a new kind of bread for the first time?

A: Meet-loaf.

Q: Why did the police arrest the chicken?

A: They suspected fowl play.

Knock knock.

Who's there?

Isaac.

Isaac who?

Isaac of these knock-knock jokes!

Q: What is a frisbee's favorite kind of music?

A: Disk-o.

Q: Why wouldn't the worm buy anything new?

A: It was dirt cheap.

Sue: Did you hear about the towel that liked to tell jokes?

Alley: Was the towel funny?

Sue: It had a dry sense of humor.

Q: Why did the pig have to sit on the bench during football practice?

A: He pulled his ham-string.

Q: What is a good thing to eat when you're feeling stressed?

A: A marsh-mellow.

Q: What kind of shoes do bakers wear?

A: Loaf-ers.

Q: What did the orange say when it was stepped on?

A: "You hurt my peelings!"

Q: Why were all the animals laughing at the owl?

A: Because he was a hoot!

Q: What do you get when you combine a monster and a genius?

A: Frank-Einstein.

Q: Why couldn't all the king's horses and all the king's men put Humpty Dumpty together again?

A: They were eggshausted.

Q: What did the composer say after the symphony?

A: "I'll be Bach."

Q: What do frogs eat on a really hot day?

A: Hop-sicles.

Q: Why did the boy always carry his piggy bank outside?

A: In case there was change in the weather.

Q: Why was the math teacher sad?

A: He had a lot of problems to solve.

Q: How did the police know the invisible man was lying?

A: They could see right through him.

Q: Why did the cat like to go bowling?

A: It was an alley cat.

Q: Why do basketball players need so many napkins?

A: They're always dribbling!

Q: Why did the bird go to the hospital?

A: To get medical tweetment.

Q: Why did the monkey go to the golf course?

A: So it could practice its swing.

Q: Where do bees go when they get married?

A: On their honey-moon.

Q: What do you call a bear with no socks?

A: Bear-foot.

Q: When can't you trust a farmer?

A: When he spills the beans!

Q: What do you call a cowboy that falls off his horse?

A: An OW-boy!

Q: Where do ducks live in the city?

A: In their pond-ominiums.

Q: What kind of animal has the best eyesight?

A: A see lion.

Q: How did the tuba call the trumpet?

A: On his saxo-phone.

Q: What do you call a really big insect?

A: A gi-ant.

Q: How did the barber win the race?

A: He took a short-cut.

Q: Where do polar bears go to vote?

A: The North Poll.

Q: What did the baby corn say to the mommy corn?

A: "Where is Pop-corn?"

Knock knock.

Who's there?

Lava.

Lava who?

I lava you!

Q: What do bumblebees play at the park?

A: Fris-bee.

Q: **Why do gorillas have big fingers?**
A: Because they have big nostrils.

Q: **What did the doe say to the fawn when it was naughty?**
A: "The buck stops here!"

Q: **Why are sheep so gullible?**
A: It's easy to pull the wool over their eyes.

Q: **What did the hat say to the scarf?**
A: "You hang around here for a while—I'm going to go ahead."

Q: **When does the alphabet only have 24 letters?**
A: When U and I are not part of it!

Q: **What kind of photographs do dentists take?**
A: Tooth pics.

Q: **When is a dinosaur boring to hang around with?**
A: When it's a dino-snore.

Q: **What happened to the cow when it lost its GPS?**
A: It became udderly lost!

Vicki: **Do you want to hear my joke about pizza?**

Leah: Not really!

Vicki: **Well, it was kind of cheesy anyway!**

Knock knock.

Who's there?

Owl.

Owl who?

Owl wait right here until you open the door!

Q: How do clams call home?

A: They use their shell phones!

Q: What do monsters sing at the ball game?

A: The national phantom.

Q: Why can't you invite pigs to your birthday party?

A: They might go hog wild.

Q: What do frogs wear in the summer time?

A: Open-toad shoes.

Q: What kind of sea creature needs help at school?

A: A "C" horse.

Q: What do you find at the end of everything?
A: The letter "g."

Q: What's brown and sticky?
A: A stick.

Q: Why are there frogs on the baseball team?
A: To catch the fly balls!

Samantha: Who stole the poor baby octopus?
   Henry: I don't know, who?
Samantha: The squidnappers!

Q: What do snowmen like best at school?
A: Snow and tell.

Q: What do you get from grumpy cows?
A: Sour milk!

Knock knock.

Who's there?

Yam.

Yam who?

I yam glad you asked—it's me!

Justin: I had a terrible dream about horses last night.

Anna: Was it a night-mare?

Q: **What do music and chickens have in common?**

A: Bach, Bach, Bach!

Q: **Why can't you win a race with a rope?**

A: It will always end with a tie.

Knock knock.

Who's there?

Butter.

Butter who?

I butter tell you a few more knock-knock jokes.

Q: **Why should you always be nice to a horse?**

A: Because you should love your neigh-bor as yourself.

Q: **Why don't you want to fight with a snail?**

A: It might try to slug you.

Knock knock.

Who's there?

Grape.

Grape who?

It would be grape if you'd tell me some more knock-knock jokes!

Q: Where does a shark go on Saturday nights?
A: To the dive-in movies.

Q: What did the girl oyster say to the boy oyster?
A: "You always clam up when I try to talk to you!"

Q: Why can't you win an argument with a pencil?
A: It's always write.

Q: What animal can jump higher than a house?
A: All of them—houses can't jump!

Q: Why couldn't the skunk go shopping?
A: It didn't have a scent in its wallet.

Q: Why did the boat go to the mall?
A: It was looking for a sail.

Q: Should we use a rowboat or a canoe to get across the lake?

A: It's either-oar.

Q: What has 50 feet and sings?

A: A choir.

Q: What do you call a cow with two legs?

A: Lean beef.

Knock knock.

Who's there?

Whale.

Whale who?

Whale you tell me another knock-knock joke?

Knock knock.

Who's there?

Gouda.

Gouda who?

Tell me another gouda knock-knock joke.

Q: Why did the people pucker up every time they drove around town?

A: Because they were driving a lemon!

Q: How can you learn more about spiders?

A: Check out their web-site.

Q: What do you call a guy stuffed in your mailbox?

A: Bill.

Josh: How do you know that eating carrots is good for your eyes?

John: Well, have you ever seen a rabbit with glasses before?

Margie: Would you like to go camping this weekend?

Minnie: No, that sounds too in-tents for me.

Q: What happens when you cross a river and a stream?

A: You get wet feet!

Q: What is smarter than a talking cat?

A: A spelling bee.

Q: Why did the bunny go to the hospital?

A: It needed a hop-eration.

Q: Why did the reporter go to the ice cream parlor?

A: He wanted to get the scoop!

Q: What is a drummer's favorite vegetable?

A: A beet.

Q: Why is it hard to carry on a conversation with rams?

A: Because they're always butting in!

Q: What kind of bear stays out in the rain?

A: A drizzly bear.

Knock knock.

Who's there?

Bean.

Bean who?

I've bean waiting for you to open the door!

Knock knock.

Who's there?

Porpoise.

Porpoise who?

Are you leaving me out here on porpoise or will you answer the door?

Knock knock.

Who's there?

Wyatt.

Wyatt who?

Wyatt is taking you so long to open the door?

Knock knock.

Who's there?

Dawn.

Dawn who?

It just Dawn-ed on me—I should tell another knock-knock joke!

Q: Why did the duck set his alarm for so early in the morning?

A: He liked to get up at the quack of dawn!

Q: What do you call a skeleton that isn't very smart?
A: A numbskull.

Q: What do you get when you cross a daisy and a bike?
A: Bicycle petals.

Knock knock.

> Who's there?

Cook.

> Cook who?

You sound a little crazy!

Knock knock.

> Who's there?

Harry.

> Harry who?

Harry up and answer the door, and I'll tell you another joke!

Q: Where can you learn to make ice cream treats?
A: In sundae school.

Q: Why don't math books last very long?

A: Their days are numbered.

Knock knock.

Who's there?

Nose.

Nose who?

Nobody nose a good joke when they hear one anymore!

Q: What do computer programmers eat when they're hungry?

A: Bytes of chips.

Q: Where do mermaids go for fun?

A: The dive-in movies!

Q: What kind of bird has a lot of money?

A: An ost-rich.

Q: Where is the best place to keep an angry dog?

A: In the grrrrage.

Q: What kind of coat is always wet and colorful?

A: A coat of paint!

Q: **Why did the bat join the circus?**

A: So it could be an acro-bat.

Knock knock.

Who's there?

Wheel.

Wheel who?

Wheel you let me tell you another knock-knock joke?

Knock knock.

Who's there?

Mark Twain.

Mark Twain who?

You mark my words, the twain will be here soon!

Q: **What kind of shoes do monsters wear?**

A: Combat boo-ts!

Q: **What do garbage collectors eat for lunch?**

A: Junk food!

Q: **What kind of bird always shows up at dinnertime?**

A: A swallow.

Q: What's a lion's favorite day of the week?
A: Chewsday.

Q: How do elk know it's hunting season?
A: They check their calen-deer!

Q: What did the snowman say to Jack Frost?
A: "Have an ice day!"

Q: What is a golfer's favorite drink?
A: Iced tee.

Q: What do you wear to play mini-golf?
A: A tee-shirt.

Q: How do porcupines stay warm in the winter?
A: They cover up with a quill-t!

Q: What kind of dogs chop down trees?
A: Lumber Jack Russells.

Knock knock.

Who's there?

Turnip.

Turnip who?

Turnip the heat—it's cold out here!

Q: What kind of cars do monsters drive?
A: Doom buggies.

Q: What did the lamb want to be when she grew up?
A: A baaaa-llerina.

Q: How can you tell when a bell is old?
A: It has ring-kles.

Q: What did the cell phone say to the landline?
A: "Hi, Grandma!"

Q: What is a rat's favorite website?
A: Mice-space.

Q: What does a clam wear to the gym?
A: A mussel shirt.

Q: Why did the snake cross the road?

A: To get to the other sssssss-ide!

Q: What is the cleanest state?

A: Wash-ington!

Knock knock.

Who's there?

Water.

Water who?

Water you doing later?

Q: What's black and white and goes around, around, and around?

A: A penguin stuck in a revolving door!

Q: Why do penguins carry fish in their beaks?

A: They don't have any pockets.

Q: What do you get when you put your notebook in your bed?

A: Sheets of paper!

Q: What do you get when you step on a piano?

A: Foot-notes!

Q: How does the snowman like his root beer?

A: In a frosted mug.

Q: What does Jack Frost call his parents?

A: Mom and Pop-sicle!

Q: Why did Frosty go live in the middle of the ocean?

A: Because snow man is an island!

Tongue Twisters

Irish wristwatch, Swiss wristwatch

Plump pink pillows

Splish splash plip plop

Coloring with crayons can cause cramps

Spunky pumpkins

Good bread, bad bread

Bouncy blue beach balls

Tickling tiny turkey toes

Crispy kitty cookies

Q: **What do you get when you hang a trumpet on a Christmas tree?**

A: A Christmas hornament.

Q: **How do crocodiles like to cook their food?**

A: In a crockpot!

Knock knock.

Who's there?

Window.

Window who?

Window we get to hear another knock-knock joke?

Wade: **What do you think of my rash?**

Merv: It's kind of gross.

Wade: **Just wait a while—it will grow on you!**

Q: **Why are possums so lazy?**

A: All they do is hang around.

Q: **Why did the billboard go to the doctor?**

A: It had a sign-us infection.

Q: What do you say to a noisy jar?

A: "Put a lid on it!"

Q: What do you get when you cross a cow and a rabbit?

A: Hare in your milk!

Q: What do get when you borrow money from a cow?

A: A buffa-loan.

Knock knock.

Who's there?

Cheryl.

Cheryl who?

Cheryl be glad to tell you another knock-knock joke!

Q: What does a carpenter eat for lunch?

A: A ham-mer and cheese sandwich.

Q: What happens when you throw your vegetables in the ocean?

A: You get sea cucumbers!

Q: Why was the cow embarrassed?

A: It had become a laughing stock.

Q: Where do musicians like to kiss?

A: Under the mistle-tone.

Q: What did the fork say to the knife?

A: "No need to be so blunt!"

Q: Why wouldn't anyone talk to the bread?

A: It was a weir-dough.

Q: Where does a horse go when it's sick?

A: To the horse-pital.

Knock knock.

Who's there?

Ache.

Ache who?

God bless you!

Q: What happened after the man accidently dropped his coffee in the volcano?

A: Java came out!

Q: What did the pen say to the pencil?

A: "Get the lead out!"

Q: What do skunks sing at Christmas time?

A: "Jingle smells, jingle smells."

Q: Why did the calendar have such a great attitude?

A: It was taking life one day at a time!

Knock knock.

Who's there?

Owl.

Owl who?

I'm owl by myself, please let me in.

Q: Why was the bird always crying?

A: Because it was a blue bird!

Q: What do bugs need to do their homework?

A: An ant-cyclopedia.

Q: What do you get when you combine an elephant and an insect?

A: An eleph-ant.

Q: What did the bread say to the baker?

A: "I need you to knead me."

Q: Why was the skeleton laughing?

A: Because he found his humerus.

Knock knock.

Who's there?

Token.

Token who?

Now that's what I'm token about!

Q: What do frogs order when they go to fast food restaurants?

A: French flies and croak-a-cola.

Anna: Was that a skeleton at the door?

Leah: No, it was no body.

Q: Why was the whale always bragging?

A: Because it was fishing for compliments.

Q: What do black bears wear in their hair?

A: Bearrettes.

Q: What kind of fish comes out at night?

A: A starfish.

Q: **What makes bananas such great drivers?**

A: They're always keeping their eyes peeled.

Q: **What did the mouse say to the rat at the movies?**

A: "The squeakuel is never as good as the original."

Q: **Why is jelly always so much fun?**

A: Because it's always jamming.

Q: **Why was the sheep practicing karate?**

A: Because it was a lamb chop!

Q: **What kind of clothing do disobedient children wear?**

A: They wear smarty-pants.

Q: **Where do fish get their money?**

A: From the loan shark.

Q: **How do ants cook their food?**

A: With a micro-wave!

Q: **How do you have a party on Mars?**

A: You have to planet.

Rob Elliott has been a publishing professional for more than twenty years and lives in West Michigan, where in his spare time he enjoys laughing out loud with his wife and five children.

Need More Laughs?

– – – – – – – – – – ✳ – – – – – – – – – –

Visit

LOLJokesForKids.com

to submit your own jokes,
receive FREE printable doodle pages,
and watch the video!

• • •

 *Laugh-Out-Loud Jokes for Kids*

 *@loljokesforkids*

Little Books,
BIG LAUGHS

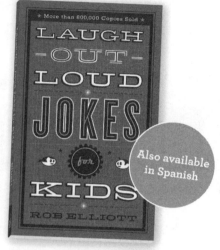

Also available in Spanish

Over 3 Million Books in the Laugh out Loud series sold